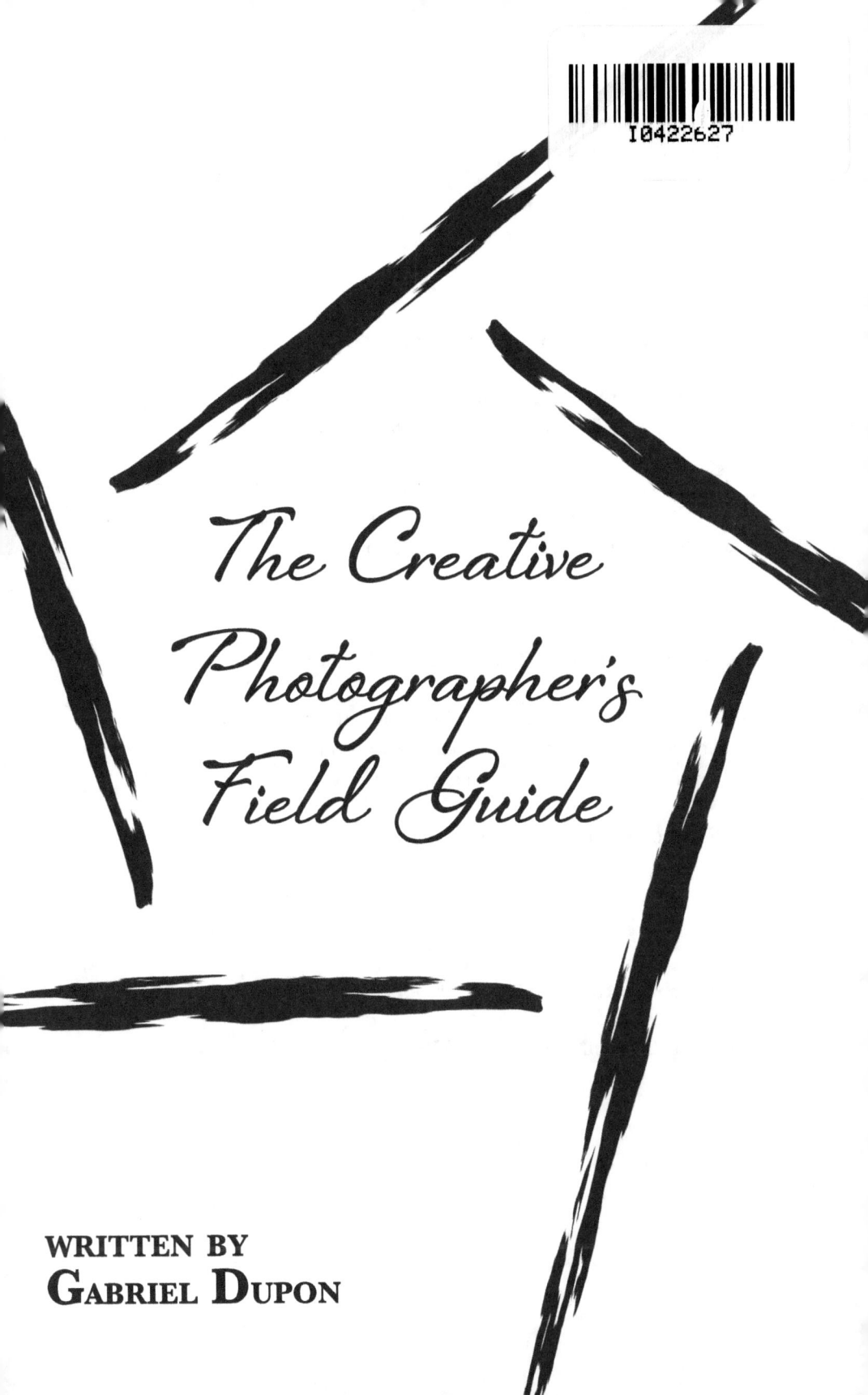

The Creative Photographer's Field Guide

WRITTEN BY
GABRIEL DUPON

Only good stuff in
here. Enjoy!

Creative contents

ARTISTRY 61

COMPOSITION 83

Dedicated to those that don't like to read much

(but also to those that like pretty books)

1

Introduction

Welcome to "The Creative Photographer's Field Guide," a book to learn and explore photography in a fun way!

In this book, there are so many topics that will elevate your skills!

To get started, read:

- Welcome photographer

- How to use this book

Welcome photographer

If there is one thing we can all agree on, life is a journey with lots of failure and success. We always strive for success but seem to be afraid to fail. If we become too fearful of failure, then we give up.

To be a successful artist, you need to take the risk by not being afraid to fail. Failure is often part of the journey to succeed, but giving up is not. Making sure you do whatever it takes to get where you want to be is a great trait to have.

Success is hard. If you want to be successful, then do it right! Of course, doing it right is a huge challenge. Especially if you consider the overwhelming amount of information available to us, it can be frustrating as an artist to read boring, lengthy books for guidance. *Why would you even want to do that?*

I wanted to change that overwhelming approach. My idea was to write an ultra-simple book with straight-to-the-point information that is fun to read! A field guide that you would bring with you on a fun vacation. A field guide to quickly reference so you can take that perfect landscape photo!

Conversely, you shouldn't expect this book to cover everything, as many topics only scratch the surface.

It's known that our reading retention rate is shallow. I created this book with many crucial digital photography topics that you can learn quickly. Each spread is structured with fundamental knowledge to help you build your own in-depth understanding.

What you learn is the ability to think independently. That is the key to capturing creative photographs!

The best way to learn photography is by going outside and experimenting with your camera, not reading books or watching tutorials. Yet, using the aid of a quick field guide (such as this book) while taking pictures can improve your craft.

Have fun creating beautiful art that you are passionate about. I hope you enjoy my book!

Sincerely,

Gabriel Dupon

"If you are going to do something, do it right, or don't do it at all!"

How to use this book

This is not a regular book; it is instead a quick reference field guide appropriate for readers of all skill levels and ages. Each spread throughout this book is a different topic to explore.

This book does not cover it all

Although this field guide covers many topics, the spreads only partially explain those topics. The reason behind this is because...

This book is for practice

The goal is to spend less time reading and more time taking pictures. Each spread should give you enough information about a topic to start figuring it out independently. This process encourages hands-on practice, which is the best way to become a better photographer.

Using the activities to grow

Each spread contains an activity box to get you started exploring the topic. These are all optional but can help you learn more about unfamiliar information related to digital photography.

5

YOUR (NEW) TRAVEL COMPANION

This is a book you can always keep in your camera bag just in case you need to reference something quickly. You never know when this field guide will be handy on a photo shoot or some grand adventure.

Imagine being on a beach vacation, and you want to take the perfect travel photos. You get caught up in the moment and forget what settings to use. Well, no need to worry. Since you brought this book along, you should have your answer within minutes!

BEST EFFORT GETS BEST RESULTS

You will get out of this book what you put into it. In other words, learning requires effort. Don't expect improvement from what you didn't practice.

If you want an easy solution to be the best imaging artist, this book won't give you that. You need to put in the effort and constantly push yourself to be the best you can be. This book only helps with the process.

Enjoy the field guide and happy shooting!

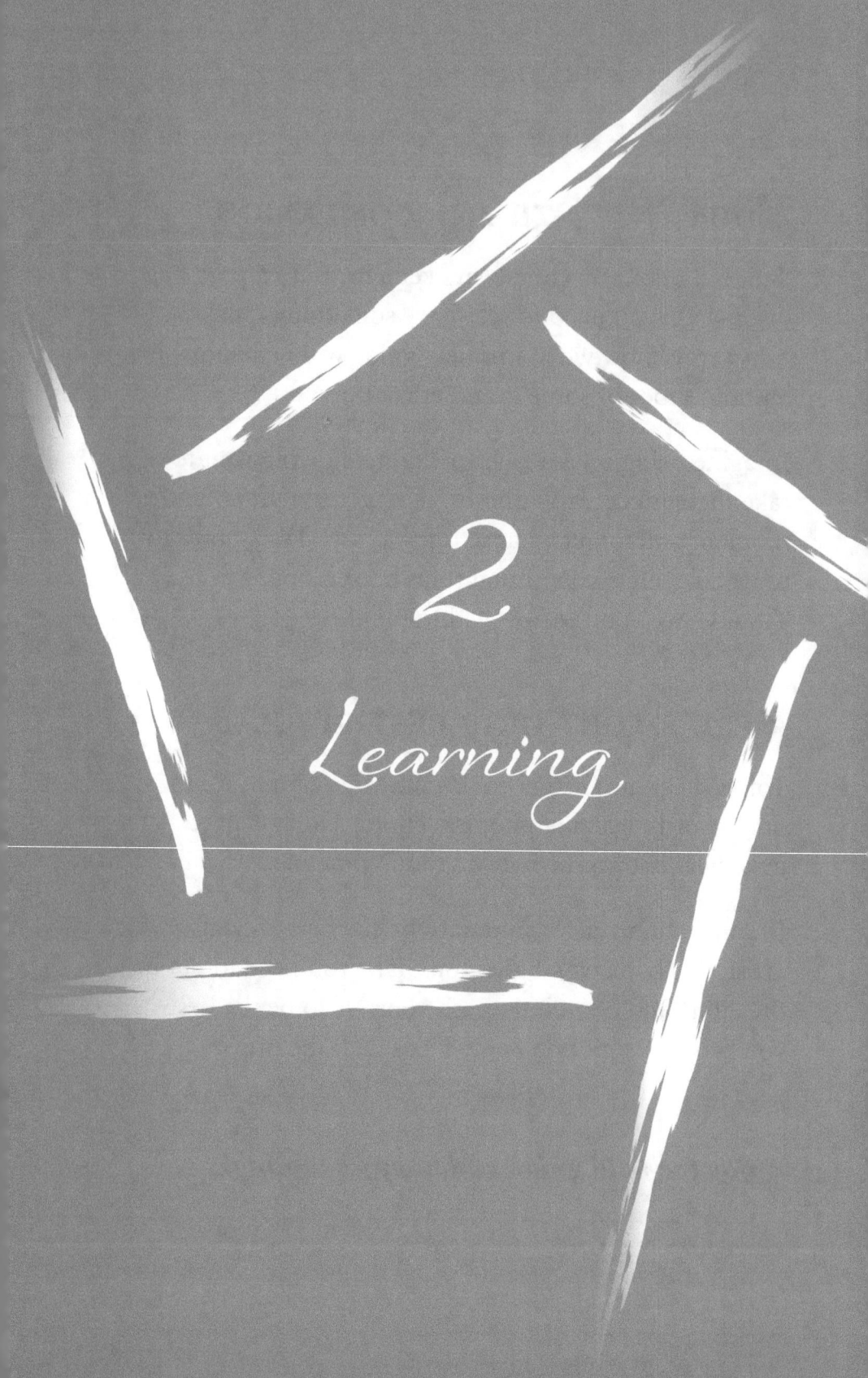

2

Learning

Knowing how to learn is the best way to set yourself up to be a successful photographer!

Before exploring the many exciting parts of this book, make sure to read:

- *Inspiration*

- *Journal*

- *Talent*

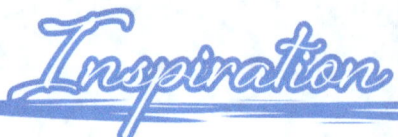

Your passion and inspiration determine a lot about the art you craft. After all, it directs you to photograph a moment.

There are two different sources of inspiration, and they play a big part in how you create a photo.

REACTIVE INSPIRATION

Inspired reactively relies on finding ideas from the work of others, such as the internet. The result images of this source are trendy and unoriginal and can make the viewers feel disconnected from your images. Reactive inspiration is often a problematic approach. Yet, this type of inspiration can still be an enjoyable way to take pictures.

PROACTIVE INSPIRATION

Inspired proactively is about pursuing your own ideas. You create these ideas from your passion and purpose for taking pictures (page 71). This source type is best if you want to create original and authentic content. However, these images may be less exciting if people expect something trendy.

Relax

Sometimes you just need to let go of whatever is on your mind and just enjoy what you are trying to accomplish.

Experiment

Force yourself to try something new and different. You may just surprise yourself with what you come up with.

No Excuses

You aren't good enough? Making excuses isn't going to make you any better. Just go out and take pictures.

Perceive

Avoid distractions such as your phone and just observe what is around you. Try to see things for what they are and appreciate them.

Ignore

Don't pay attention to what others are saying or doing. If others don't like your photography, just ignore those people.

Photography inspiration model that you can use to innovate your craft.

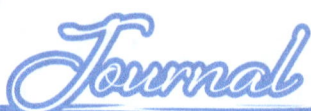

As you explore new ways to take pictures and travel to novel places, you should journal. Spending time to reflect on what you did also works since traditional journaling isn't required.

REFLECTION

Spend time doing something where you can think about what you did correctly and how you can improve. Reflection can be simply sitting down and writing it out. Or by thinking about it as you do a physical activity you enjoy. There is no right or wrong way to reflect; do whatever works best for you!

ACTIVITIES

All the spreads throughout this book contain an activity box to assist you in becoming better. These activities are to help you start exploring a topic, so customize, experiment, and revisit them as much as you can. The more you can challenge yourself, the better!

If you want to keep track of these activities, you can use the "activities log" in the appendix at the end of this book (page 121). You can also mark a star in this log once you've challenged yourself significantly.

METADATA

Pay attention to your exposure details, capture time, lens used, and other shooting information. Metadata can be very helpful for learning purposes when going through your pictures.

Looking at your metadata allows you to become aware of what settings you used. This practice encourages you to understand what worked and what didn't work.

PHOTO LIBRARY

As you take thousands of pictures, organize them in your library. Doing this lets you look back at your pictures and easily find them. Organize your pictures by year, month, and day. Here is an example of using hierarchy folder-based organization.

📁 **Year** *(e.g., 2024 Photo Library)*
  📁 **Month** *(e.g., 02 - February 2024)*
    📁 **Day** *(e.g., February 29)*

Once you do a trip or a photo shoot, add those pictures into collections or albums. If you fall in love with a specific picture that you captured, make sure to flag, heart, or give it a star rating. You can also add tags or labels if that's your style.

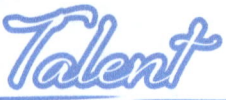

If your eyes are looking at this book, then it is clear that you want to take better pictures.

Here's some advice if you desire to become the best photographer you can!

REMEMBER: YOU ARE THE ARTIST

A better camera does not mean better pictures. It can help, but you shouldn't ever rely on it. Besides, fancier cameras have more features that you probably don't need. Remember, you are the artist:

> *"Photographers are like musicians. The instruments they use don't produce their work, but rather the artist."*

CREATE GOALS

Setting goals is a great way to improve at anything you do, including photography. As you read this, write down an attainable goal that you want to achieve on a sticky note or your bookmark. Additionally, complete all of the activities on each spread as micro goals to help reinforce your main goal!

Deliberate practice

A great way to become your best is to be in a constant uncomfortable state of doing complex challenges. Be aware that once you become comfortable with easy practice, you won't be improving anymore. On the flip side, if you are challenging yourself to an extreme level, don't expect to improve either.

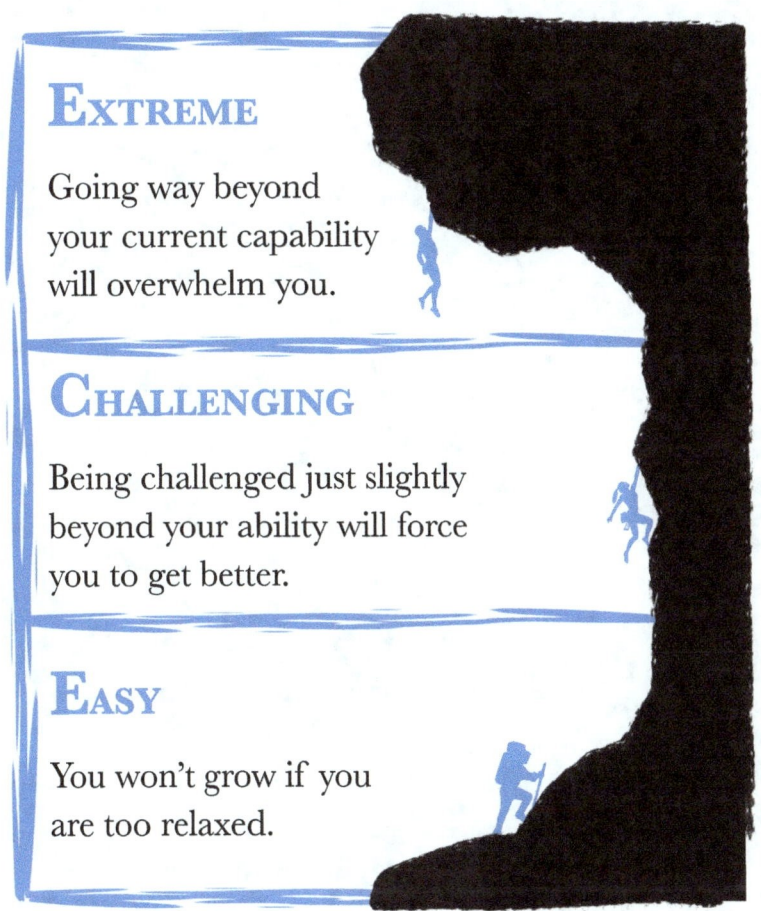

Extreme

Going way beyond your current capability will overwhelm you.

Challenging

Being challenged just slightly beyond your ability will force you to get better.

Easy

You won't grow if you are too relaxed.

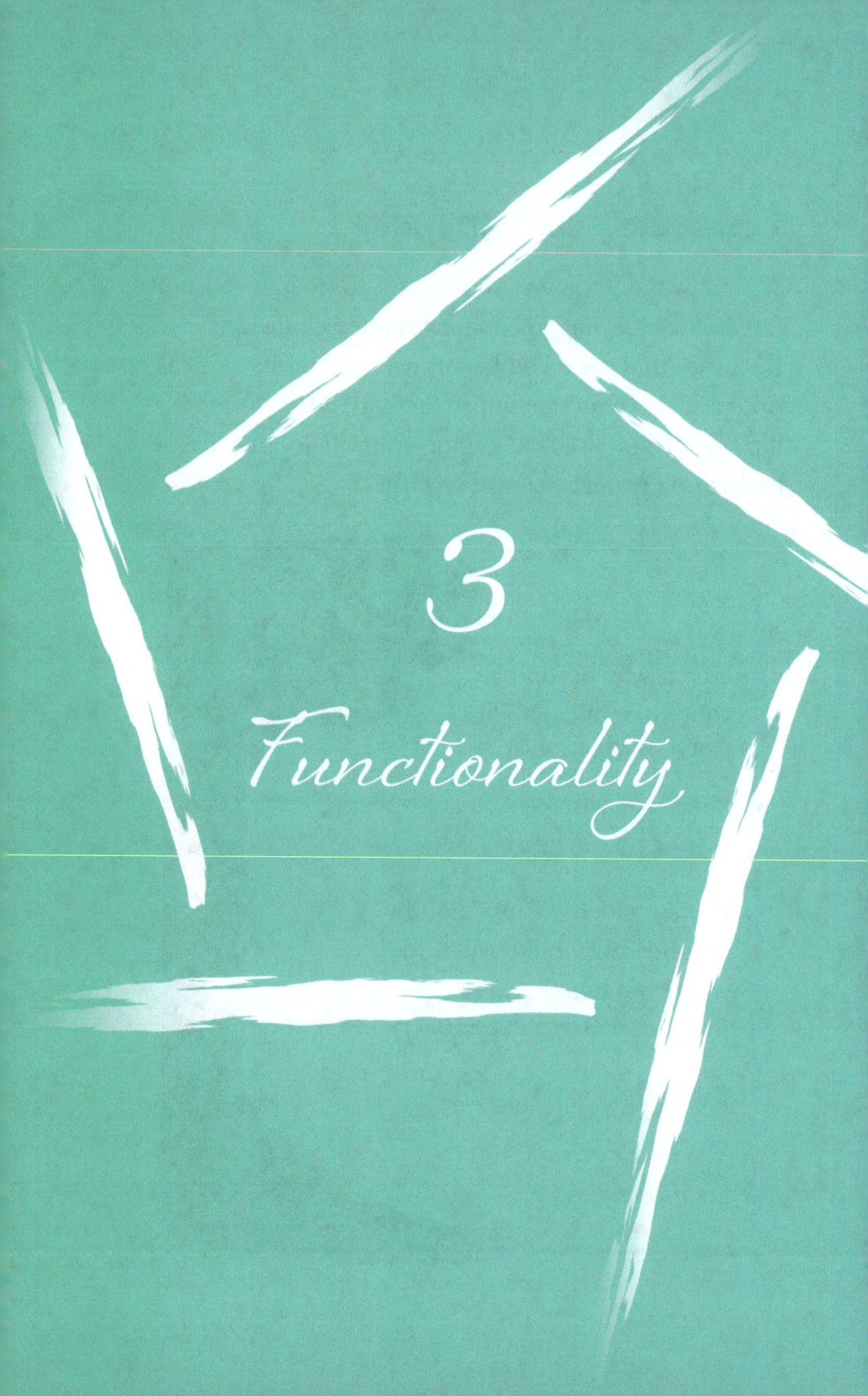

3

Functionality

To use your camera effectively and efficiently, you need to understand all of the functions.

This knowledge will allow you to experiment and have lots of fun! All of the functions include:

- *Camera anatomy*

- *Metering modes*

- *Shooting modes*

- *Focusing modes*

- *Release modes*

- *Customization*

- *Composites*

- *Remote*

Camera anatomy

Knowing what each part of your camera is and what each button does is essential to using your camera. Every camera is different, but they all have the same primary functions. Look at your camera manual for the parts specific to your brand and model.

THE MAIN PARTS OF THE CAMERA

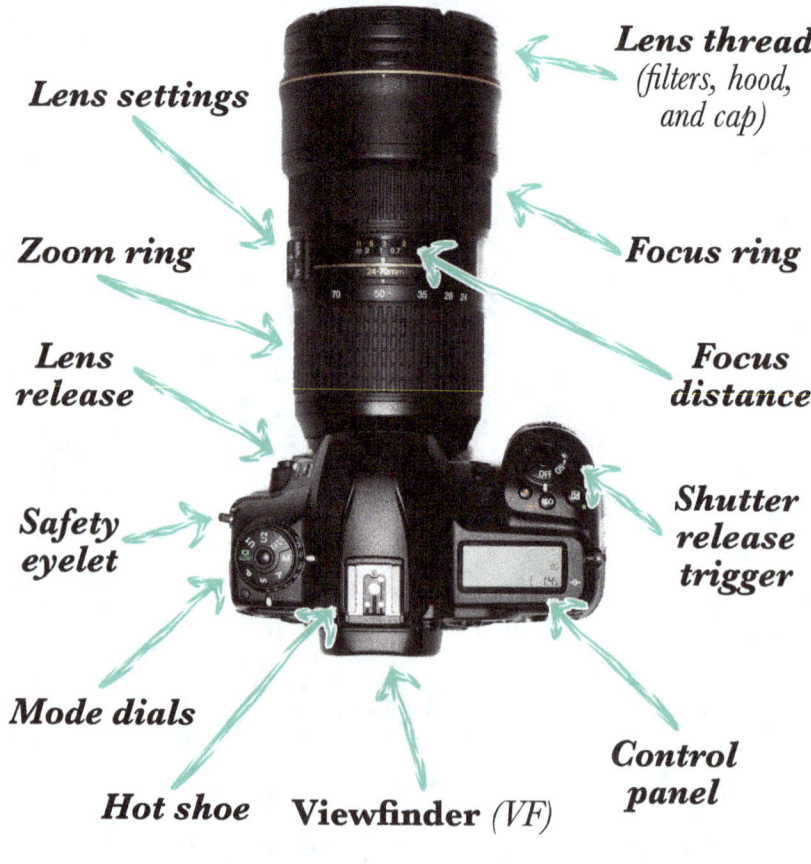

Lens thread
(filters, hood, and cap)

Lens settings

Zoom ring

Focus ring

Lens release

Focus distance

Safety eyelet

Shutter release trigger

Mode dials

Hot shoe *Viewfinder* (VF)

Control panel

(Underneath camera: 1/4"-20 socket for tripod mounting)

THE MAIN CONTROLS OF THE CAMERA

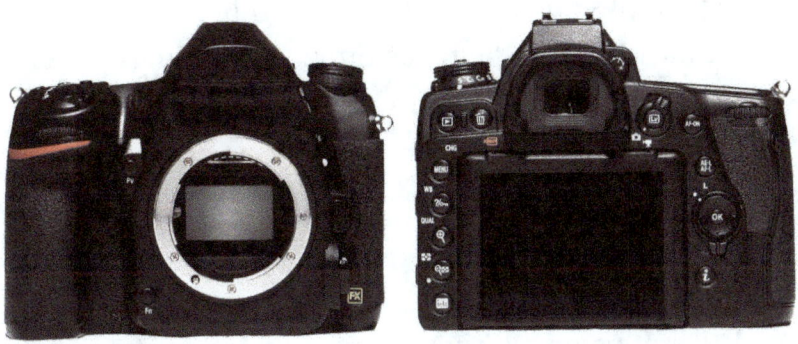

Control dials and thumb pad - modify aperture, shutter speed, focus points, and menu navigation. They can also change ISO, white balance, focus modes, and metering modes when you press the appropriate button.

Standard controls - you will find a button or switch for autofocus, playback, delete, live view, AE/AF lock, VF diopter adjustment, menu, info, quality, aperture preview, and functions you can program (page 27).

Activity #1

Look for all the parts/functions (mentioned in this spread) on your camera. Try all of the buttons and dials to discover what each function does.

Metering modes

Your camera uses different methods of measuring light through the lens. The metering can help set the exposure settings automatically. They can also display an indication to help customize the settings when shooting with manual mode (page 21).

▣ EVALUATIVE / MATRIX

Evaluative or matrix measures the intensity of light from divided zones. This metering option is the best choice to find the most balanced exposure across the entire image. It is the default and most popular metering option.

▣ CENTER-WEIGHTED

Center-weighted metering excludes the peripheral area of the image. This metering method also becomes progressively more sensitive towards the center.

▣ SPOT

Spot only measures the light in a small dot at the center or a specific focus point within the viewfinder. Some cameras may also have "partial" metering, an option with a larger dot.

Exposure indicator

When shooting in manual or priority mode, the exposure indicator can help you get accurate exposure. The indicator will point to an area on the chart (shown below) to tell you whether your chosen camera settings will underexpose ("**-**"), overexpose ("**+**"), or accurately expose ("**O**") the image.

- **|** . . **|** . . **|** . . **|** . . **|** . . **|** . . **|** +

A meter indication will be determined based on your chosen metering mode and the amount of grayness in the image. Because of this, the meter can get confused when taking pictures of a black or a white object.

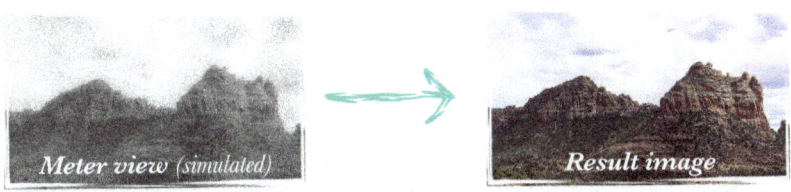

Meter view (simulated) → *Result image*

Activity #2

Experiment with different metering modes on various subjects with diverse lighting situations. Do this to discover how your camera meters the light.

Shooting modes

The ultimate mode of your camera controls how you can change necessary settings when taking pictures. The following four modes are essential to learn if you want to master exposure.

M - MANUAL

Manual mode allows you to adjust all the setting freely. You must use the exposure indicator from your chosen metering mode to help you (page 19).

Av/A - APERTURE PRIORITY

Aperture priority mode allows you only to adjust the aperture value. Everything else will be set automatically.

Tv/S - SHUTTER SPEED PRIORITY

Shutter speed priority mode lets you only adjust the exposure time value. Everything else will be set as auto.

P - PROGRAM AUTO

Program auto is entirely automatic, except you can use "exposure values" (EV) to increase or decrease the brightness.

Exposure triangle

Use the exposure triangle as a reference to help you achieve accurate exposure. To learn more about each setting, go to the exposure section on page 53.

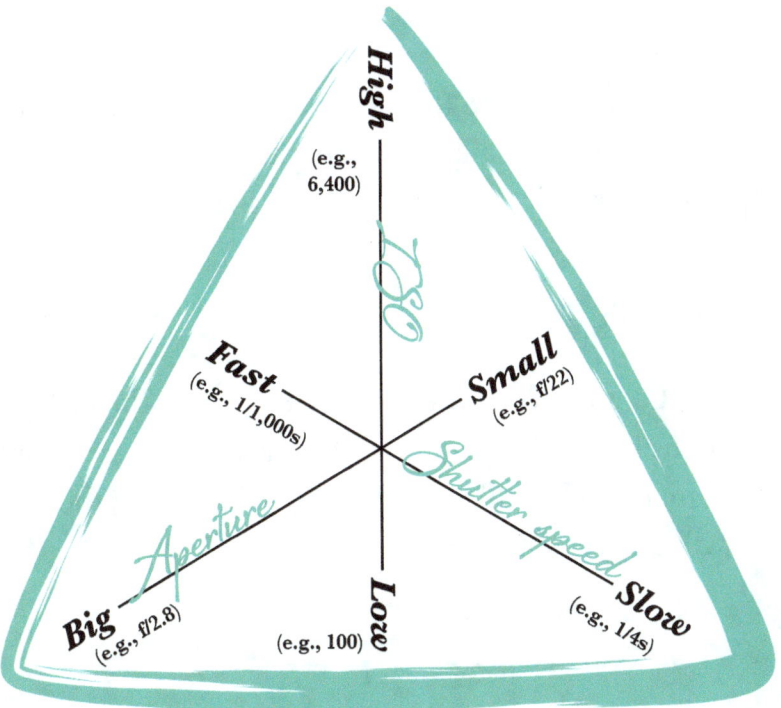

Activity #3

Go on a walk and take pictures using "manual" or a priority mode. Challenge yourself to get the exposure as accurate as possible.

Focusing modes

Various focusing modes can help you adjust the lens focus. These modes ensure you efficiently capture perfectly focused images without missing a moment.

Autofocus - single servo (AF-S)

AF-S freezes once the camera confirms that the object is in focus. Usually, the camera will prevent you from taking any pictures until it locks focus.

Autofocus - continuous (AF-C)

AF-C only stops when you release your finger from the focus button. Otherwise, the camera will be constantly refocusing. Unlike "single servo," pressing the trigger will always activate the shutter.

Manual focus (MF)

Change to manual focus mode and rotate the focus ring on your lens. You can use the distance markers on your lens by matching the measurement from an object to the focal plane mark (—⊖—) on your camera.

Also, some cameras have a feature called "focus assist" that indicates what you have in focus.

AUTOFOCUS AREA OPTIONS

When using an autofocus mode, you also need to choose a method for focus point selection.

[⊏⊐] **Single point (s)** - choose the exact point you want the camera to focus on. Option "**s**" is the most precise but is also the least efficient to use.

[⊏⊐] **Dynamic-area (d)** - similar to "single point," except if the subject moves away, the camera will adjust within the area of a specific amount of "**d**" points.

[3D] **Tracking** - select an object (such as an eye) with a single point, and the camera will track the movements.

[▬] **Auto** - the camera identifies unique features such as faces and high contrast points.

Activity #4

Try the different focusing modes to find the one you are most comfortable using. Make sure you try photographing both still and high-speed subjects. *(Tip: if your camera allows, change the custom settings to enable back button focusing).*

Release modes

The release modes can determine how the shutter is activated when you press the release button trigger.

SINGLE FRAME

Single is the default mode, capturing only one photograph as you press the release trigger.

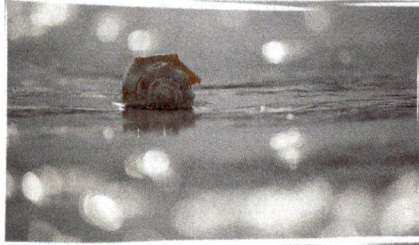

Use "single frame" for shooting subjects that are static or don't move quickly.

CONTINUOUS SHOOTING

Hold down on the trigger, and your camera will start taking pictures rapidly without stopping. There is usually a low-fps (frames-per-second) and a high-fps option for this mode.

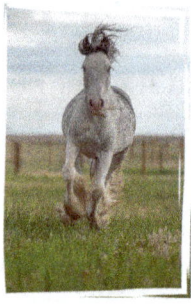

Use "continuous shooting" for subjects that move quickly, such as animals and sports. This mode ensures that you are more likely to capture the right moment.

Quiet shutter

For moments that require you to be silent, you can set the camera to decrease and sometimes eliminate sounds caused by the camera's operation.

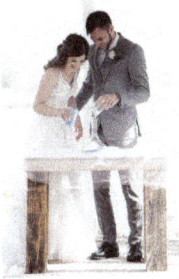

Use a "quiet shutter" when you need to be discrete, such as at a wedding ceremony. This mode allows you to be non-obtrusive during special moments.

Timer delay

Set the camera to take a picture after a certain amount of time (e.g., 10 seconds) once you press the trigger.

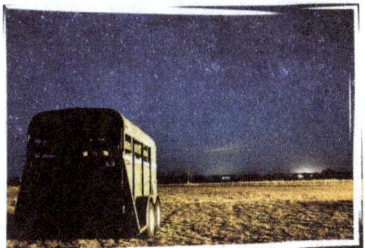

Use "timer delay" for self-portraits or to minimize vibrations for long-exposure photos.

Activity #5

Use all the different release modes on a variety of situations and subjects. What worked best for you?

Customization

You can go through your camera's functions and customize them. Doing this allows you to be more efficient and makes taking pictures easier.

Setup menus

Add your copyright information and select the "time zone and date." You can also choose your "color control profile" (page 39) and "file format" (page 43).

Custom settings

Custom settings in the menu allow you to change the camera's default system. These settings can help you take full advantage of a camera's features and usability.

Function buttons

Inside the setup or custom settings menu, you can program buttons. You can repurpose or swap buttons on your camera to better suit your shooting style. A popular button modification is to enable back button focusing so you can use your thumb to autofocus instead of your index finger.

CREATE A CUSTOM MENU

Some cameras allow you to create a "my menu" with items found throughout the entire menu database. Creating this enables you to quickly access menu items in one convenient place. Check out the example below of what your customized menu could look like.

	MY MENU	
	White balance	K
E	ISO settings	100
X	Active D-lighting	LOW
A		
M	High ISO noise reduction	NORM
P	Set picture control	SD
L		
E	Battery info	36%
	Image quality	RAW
	Bluetooth	OFF

Activity #6

Go through your camera's menus and find settings that you are unfamiliar with. Experiment with those settings to find what you like and don't like. Also, go through your camera's "custom settings" and "setup menu" to customize your camera.

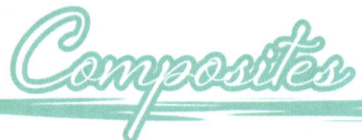

Composites

It is possible to merge many pictures into one image. Compositing allows you to create an image that would be impossible to achieve with a single photo.

Bracketing

When shooting landscapes and real estate, bracketing can help you achieve a "high dynamic range" (HDR) image. Bracketing is a feature in your camera, which takes a series of pictures all at different settings.

Bracketing exposure is most common, but you can also bracket white balance, flash, and focus. You can merge these photos in a computer application to create a dynamic image. This process allows you to keep the most balanced or best parts of each image.

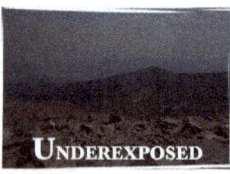
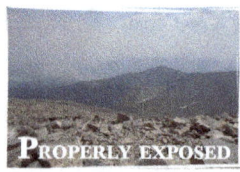
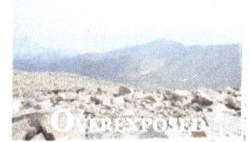

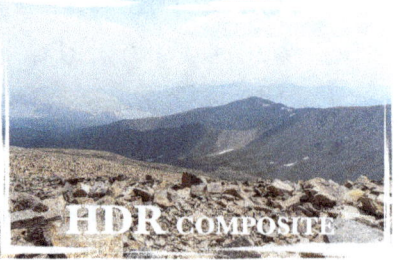

Panorama

You can create a panorama by using a merge tool in your editor. All you need to do is shoot several pictures of a scene that are all slightly overlapping each other.

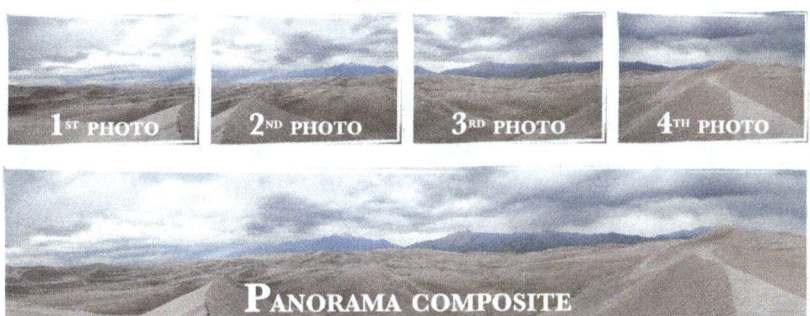

Multiple exposure

Combining the exposures of several pictures within one image is known as a multiple exposure. Many cameras have this function found in the menu.

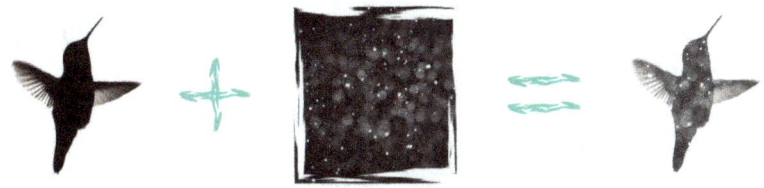

Activity #7

Try one or all of the composite methods on this spread. Experiment with different techniques to find your favorite way to achieve a fascinating photograph.

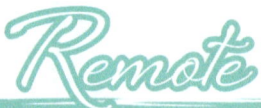

During particular circumstances, you may need to operate your camera remotely. A remote could allow you to achieve the best photo possible.

WIRELESS SHOOTING

Using a remote is a great way to take pictures without being by your camera. It is also a way to reduce any vibrations during long exposures because you won't be touching the camera. To do this, you can either use your mobile phone via Bluetooth or a radio/infrared remote control.

INTERVALOMETER SHOOTING

Use an intervalometer remote or the interval settings in your camera. Doing this enables you to take many pictures over a specific amount of time.

Interval shooting can be helpful to create a time-lapse or to capture moments you can't precisely predict, such as lightning. It won't guarantee to capture what you want, but it does significantly increase your odds.

To set your intervalometer settings, you must schedule an interval duration (the time between each shot) and the total shooting duration.

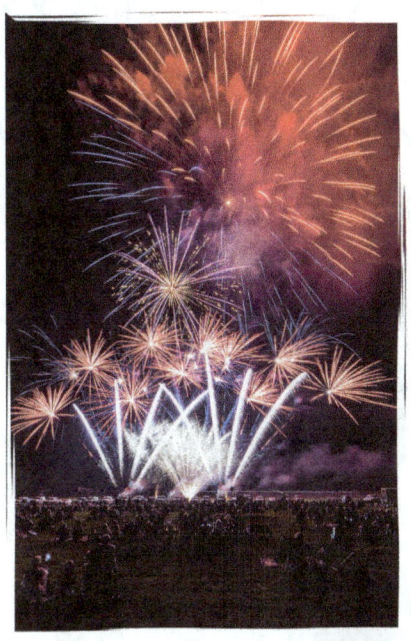

Using a remote can be a great way to trigger the shutter while enjoying an event such as a fireworks display.

For example, you can set your camera on a tripod and use your phone to release and un-release a bulb shutter.

You may take hundreds of pictures to get a few great shots, but it is worth it!

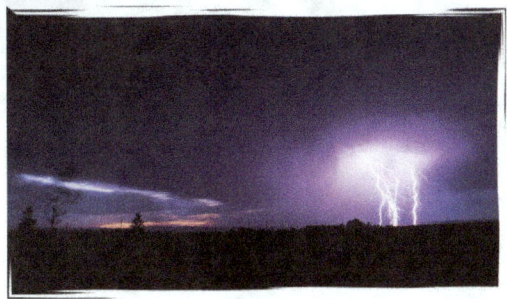

Activity #8

Set up an interval on your camera to create a time-lapse movie, lightning photo, or a star-trails image. Also, try triggering the shutter wirelessly next time you attempt a long exposure image.

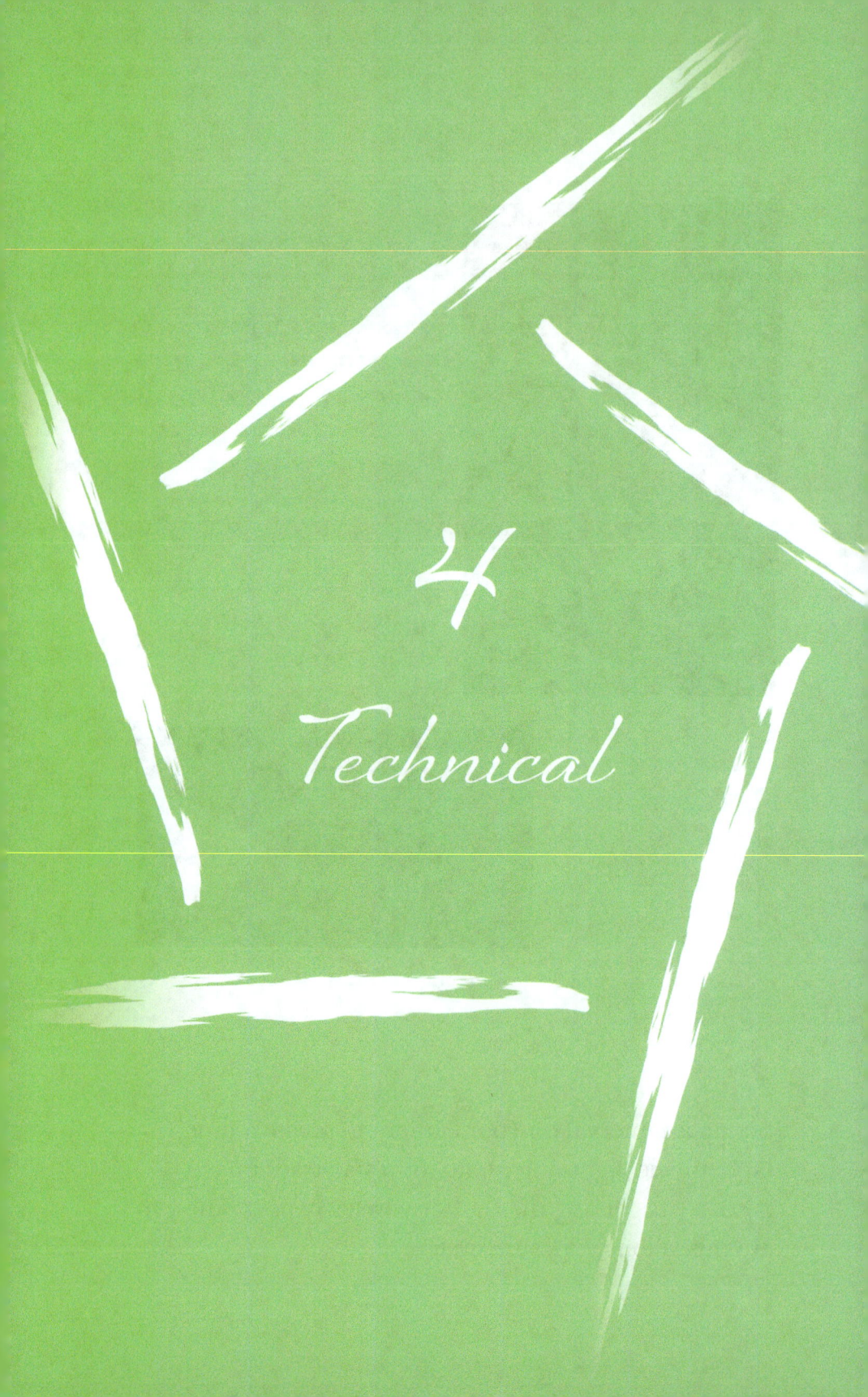

4

Technical

Understanding the technical parts of photography may be less fun, but it will help you create the best images possible.

All of this includes:

- *Memory cards*

- *White balance*

- *Color profiles*

- *Camera care*

- *File formats*

- *Image area*

- *Resolution*

- *Support*

- *Filters*

Memory cards

Without a CF or SD card, it would be impossible to save the pictures you capture. Ensure you use memory cards properly, and it will save you a headache later on.

FORMATTING CARDS

To avoid problems, use the camera to format new memory cards before taking pictures. Formatting allows the card to ignore the existence of current data so you can capture new pictures. You should also re-format the memory cards once you safely store the pictures in your photo library (page 107).

DELETING PICTURES

It is a discouraged practice to delete pictures in-camera as this can increase the chance of your card becoming corrupted. If you need to remove a picture, wait until you import them into your computer.

DUAL CARD SLOTS

If your camera supports dual card slots, you are encouraged to take advantage of it. Set your second slot to "backup role" to safeguard your pictures in case something terrible happens to one of the cards.

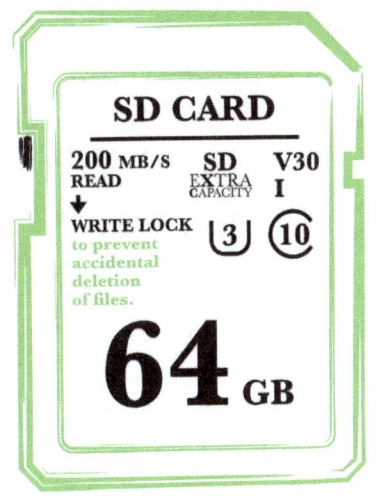

MINIMUM WRITE SPEED	CLASSIFICATION
6 MB/S	C6 / V6
10 MB/S	C10 / V10 / U1
30 MB/S	V30 / U3
60 MB/S	V60
90 MB/S	V90

CARD SIZE AND SPEED

The speed and size of a memory card aren't very critical unless you are shooting high-quality video or raw photo bursts.

It is a good idea to have a few 32GB (SDHC) or 64GB (SDXC) memory cards that are at least UHS-I / V30 / U3 (minimum sequential write speed of 30mb/s), such as the example above. This specification of a memory card should be sufficient for most types of photography.

Activity #9

Make sure that you have quality memory cards and an established workflow. A workflow helps avoid mishaps such as corruption or losing a card.

White balance

Setting the white balance will ensure your pictures' colors are pleasing and believable to the eye. Your goal is to choose a color temperature that appears the most natural for the scene.

COLOR TEMPERATURE

Color temperature is measured in Kelvin and consists of blues and ambers. Most cameras have auto and built-in preset options that match the white balance to the light source. However, if you want to adjust the white balance manually, choose the K option.

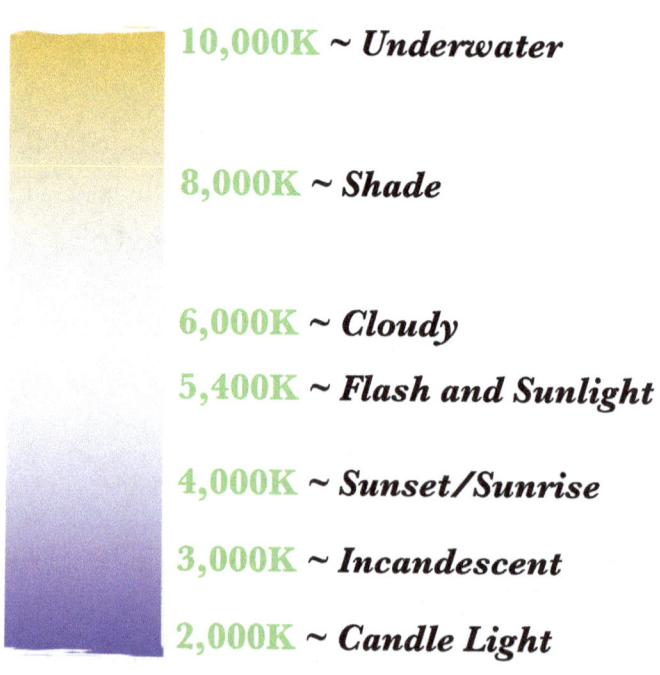

10,000K ~ *Underwater*

8,000K ~ *Shade*

6,000K ~ *Cloudy*

5,400K ~ *Flash and Sunlight*

4,000K ~ *Sunset/Sunrise*

3,000K ~ *Incandescent*

2,000K ~ *Candle Light*

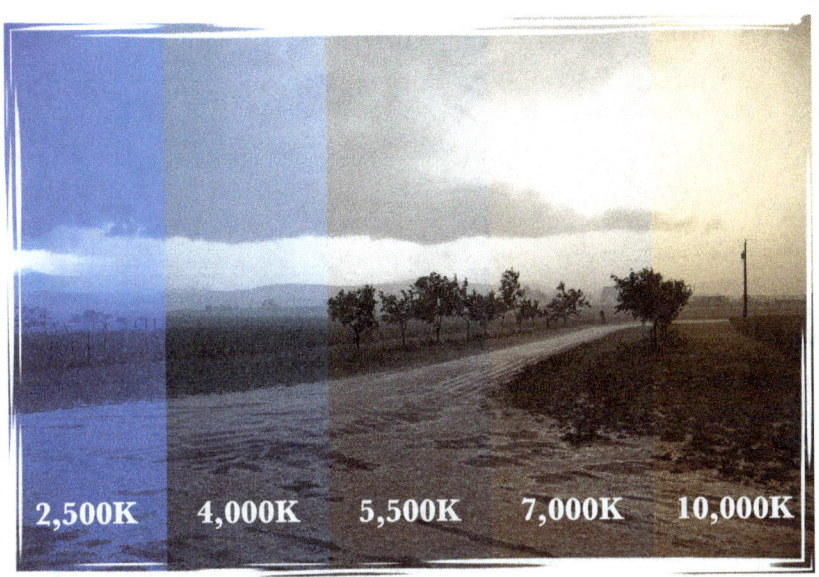

2,500K 4,000K 5,500K 7,000K 10,000K

White balance is not only limited to adjusting before capturing a photo. If you take pictures in RAW format (page 43), you can adjust the white balance of your pictures with an editing application.

Activity #10

Take pictures of subjects with various light sources and choose a different color temperature for each picture. Compare the differences and find the one you like the best or appears the most natural.

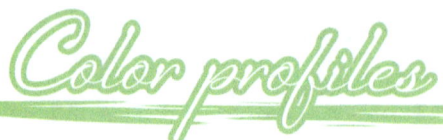

Color profile settings allow you to set how you want the camera to process the colors as you take pictures.

COLOR SPACE

Choose how each picture defines color. Options are usually available as:

sRGB: *best if you don't want to edit*

AdobeRGB: *best if you plan to edit*

COLOR CONTROL

The pictures your camera takes are usually quite generic-looking. They will need to be processed depending on how you use the image.

Flat: *preserves details in the tonal range*

Vivid/Landscape: *enhanced coloring*

Portrait: *soft skin tone coloring*

Monochrome: *black and white*

Neutral: *minimal processing*

Standard: *balanced coloring*

Some cameras may also allow you to make custom color control profiles.

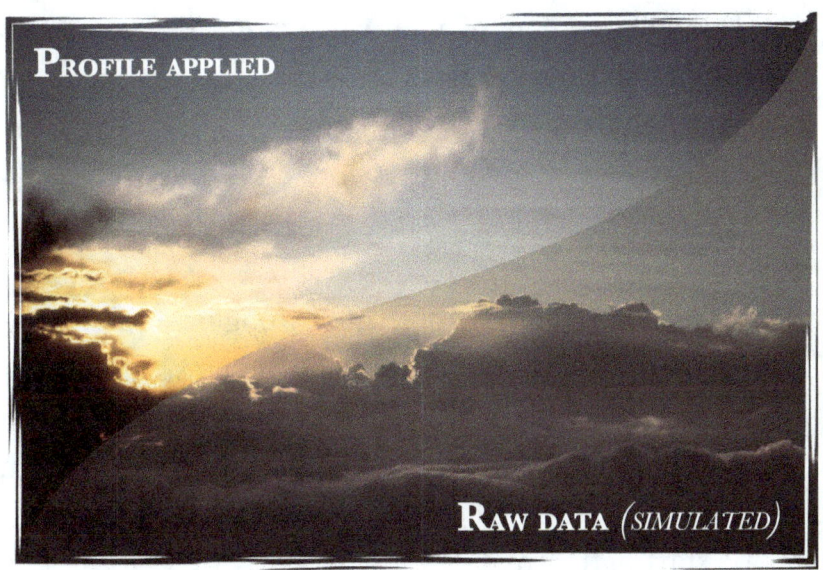

PROFILE APPLIED

RAW DATA *(SIMULATED)*

As you can see, the look of raw data isn't as attractive. By selecting the color space and color control profile, you can make your image stand out! If you capture your image in RAW format, you can change the profile when you edit the image.

Activity #11

Take multiple pictures of the same object, each with a different color profile. Repeat this with many subjects and lighting conditions. Once finished, compare the results and find the one you like best!

Camera care

Taking good care of your camera ensures you can stay taking pictures for many years.

AVOIDING MOISTURE

Water is a massive problem for imaging equipment. It can cause corrosion, electrical problems, and fungus to grow. To avoid these problems, store your equipment with desiccant and regularly use each lens outside in the sun. Tip: ultraviolet light can kill anything that might be starting to grow.

PHYSICAL DAMAGE

Murphy's Law is that whatever can happen will happen. This reason is why using quality camera straps or having equipment insurance is a good idea.

Many photographers also like to use UV filters (page 51) on their lenses to help protect them, but two problems are associated with this. UV filters don't allow you to take advantage of the premium coatings on your lens, and they block ultraviolet light, which is essential to kill fungal growth.

An alternative is to always use the hood, as this will best protect your lens. Plus, it will also reduce lens flares.

Cleaning the lens

Your lens will often get smudges, preventing you from getting clear images. To clean your lens, spray lens cleaner on a microfiber cloth and gradually wipe in a circular motion from the center to the edges.

Cleaning the sensor

Neglecting to clean your camera's sensor will inevitably bring dirt spots on your photos. To regularly clean your sensor or low-pass filter, use a "clean air dust-removal tool" to blow air into your camera safely. You can blow air straight into a mirrorless camera, but for a DSLR, you will need to lock the mirror up.

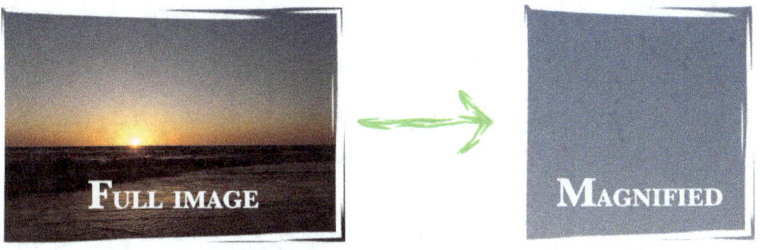

Activity #12

Build a habit of regularly cleaning your camera before taking pictures. Maintaining your camera will ensure you stay satisfied with everything working correctly.

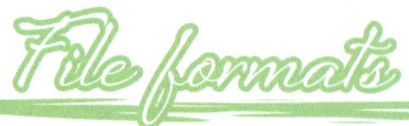

File formats

Each picture you take is a container of data put into a specific format that is readable by computers. The most common file formats for photography include JPEG and RAW.

JPEG

JPEG file format is widely accepted, compressed for small file sizes, and contains nearly 16.8 million colors (8-bits). Fun fact: JPEG stands for "**J**oint **P**hotographic **E**xperts **G**roup."

RAW

RAW can be a variety of container files such as NEF, CR2, ARW, or DNG. The ability to shoot RAW provides flexibility for editing your pictures (page 95) as they will contain more colors than JPEG.

12-bit RAW ≈ *68.7 billion colors*

14-bit RAW ≈ *4.4 trillion colors*

16-bit RAW ≈ *281.5 trillion colors*

The massive amount of colors permits you to adjust the white balance, color profiles, and exposure values after capturing the photograph.

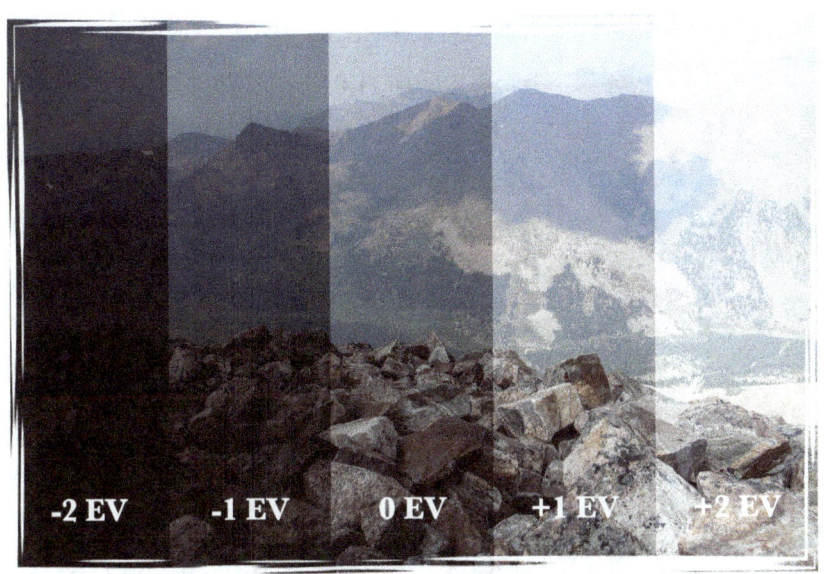

-2 EV   -1 EV   0 EV   +1 EV   +2 EV

Example of the dynamic range when post-adjusting exposure values of an image captured in 14-bit RAW. Look on page 37 for an example of how you can also post-adjust the white balance. Additionally, look on page 39 for how you can post-change color profiles.

Activity #13

Take a series of pictures of the same scene with different exposure values in both JPEG and RAW. Edit each set of pictures and compare the differences. Also, post-adjust the white balance and color profiles to compare those differences.

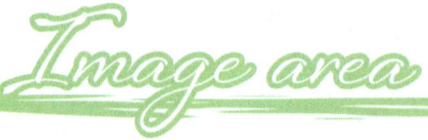 Image area

The image area is the crop factor of your camera's sensor. Each camera will have a different sensor size. There are advantages to each size, but there is never a limit to capturing beautiful images.

SIZE DIFFERENCE

Although all sensor sizes do the same job, the size of the sensor does affect the quality of the photo. The benefits of a larger sensor enable the camera to capture more light and detail, creating a more immersive image. However, the benefits of a smaller sensor are affordability and faster shutter speeds.

PHOTOSITES

A larger sensor doesn't necessarily mean more resolution (page 47). For example, suppose an APS-C and a full-frame sensor can capture 24 megapixels. In that case, the full-frame sensor will likely have bigger photosites.

A photosite is a micro sensor that receives the color and light for a single pixel. Larger photosites can perform better, recording data more accurately at higher ISO values (page 59).

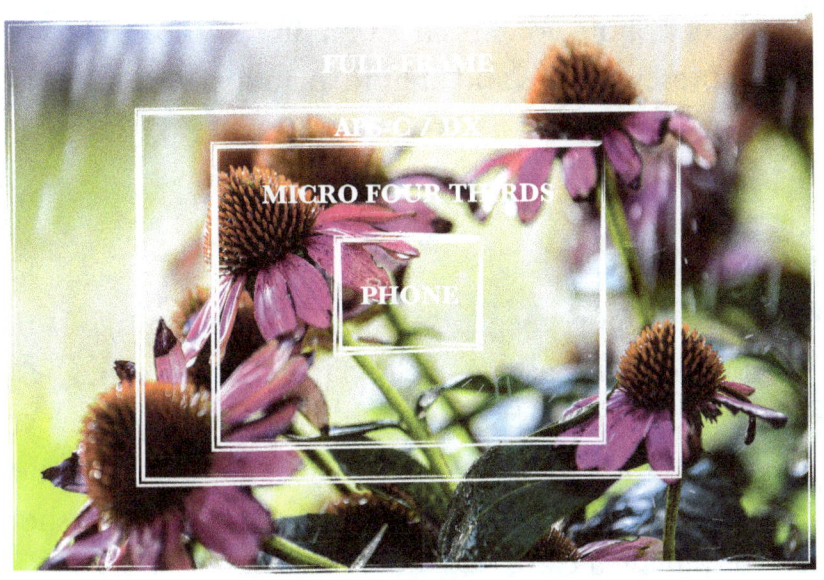

Full-frame ≈ *36x24mm (x1 crop)*

APS-C / DX ≈ *24x16mm (x1.5 crop)*

Micro Four Thirds (MFT) ≈ *17x13mm (x2 crop)*

Mobile phone sensor ≈ *7.8x5.8mm (x4.5 crop)*

Activity #14

Access multiple cameras with different sensor sizes (such as a phone camera and a DSLR). Take pictures of the same subject with each camera and compare the results. What do you notice differently?

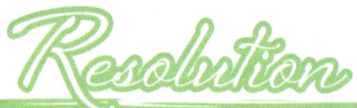

Resolution

Every photo contains a set amount of pixels that represent colors and light to form a picture.

Benefits

Having more megapixels (one million pixels) is better, but you must ask yourself, "How much is enough?" All you need is 4K, but since most cameras allow you to shoot 6K+, you can crop (page 105). Here are the resolution tiers that you can choose from when shooting or buying a camera.

2K ≈ 3mp (mobile screens, small prints)

4K ≈ 11mp (monitors, medium prints)

6K ≈ 24mp (cropping, large prints)

8K ≈ 43mp (cinema, cropping, huge prints)

Drawbacks

Desiring higher-resolution images isn't always a good thing. Increasing megapixels will have the following issues: requires higher definition lenses with a precise focusing mechanism, bigger file sizes, a faster shutter speed, and sometimes will also capture details you wouldn't otherwise want to see.

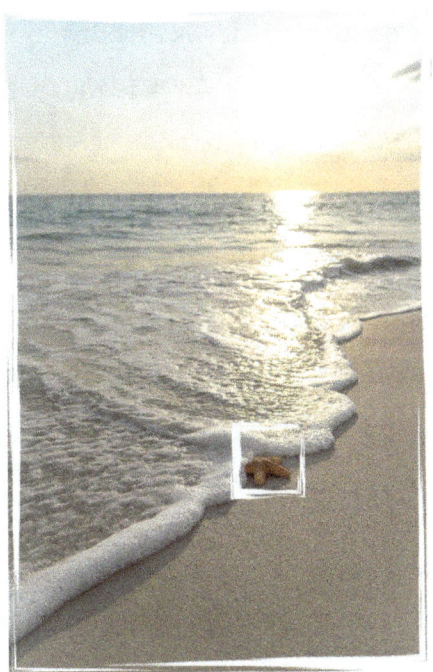
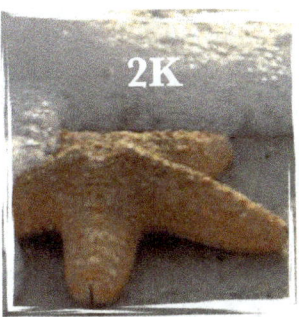
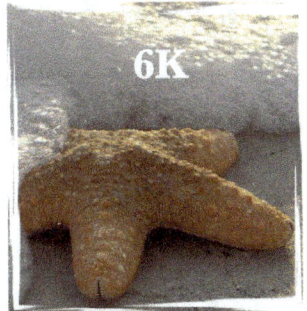

The above example demonstrates why resolution is vital
by comparing the difference between 2K and 6K.
It allows you to see more texture and details, which
helps the viewers immerse themselves in the image.

Activity #15

Find some of your favorite images and make digital
copies of them. For each copy, resize them at different
resolutions and compare them against each other.
How much did the quality of your images change?

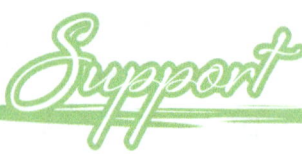

Securing your camera or accessories is essential for safety and for capturing specific types of photos.

HAND-HOLDING YOUR CAMERA

Before you take a picture, know how to hold your camera steady by following these steps.

Feet: *have a solid and balanced stance.*

Elbows: *keep your elbows tucked in.*

Hands: *support the camera with your right hand, and the lens with your left hand.*

Breathing: *pay attention to your breathing and push the trigger once you are steady.*

EXTERNAL SUPPORT

If you need to keep your camera steady for prolonged shutter speeds (page 55) or you want to reduce body strain, externally supporting your camera is essential. You can use supports such as a tripod, monopod, rig, or a clamp. Note that the steadiness of a tripod could confuse image stabilization (IS) or vibration reduction (VR) systems, so you will need to deactivate them.

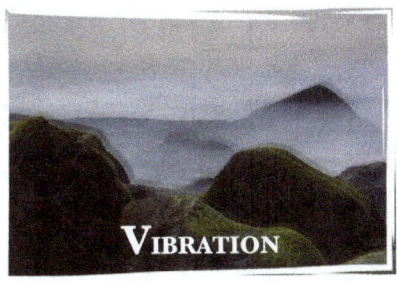

VIBRATION

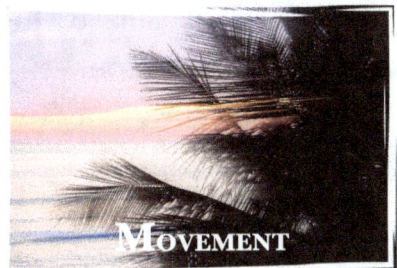

MOVEMENT

Above are examples of camera shake caused by vibration and movement. This outcome happens when you don't correctly support and stabilize your camera during telephoto or long-exposure photos.

The slower the shutter speed and longer the focal length, the more susceptible your images will be to camera shake (ghosting effect) and motion blur.

Support is a technical aspect of photography, but you can use it creatively if you desire an unstable look. Intentionally panning images during your exposure time can create unique effects.

Activity #16

Practice taking pictures handheld with a shutter speed of 1/30th or slower. Discover what keeps the camera steady for a sharp image without any camera shake. Also, experiment by intentionally causing motion blur in some of your images.

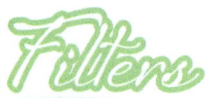

Attach specialized filters to your lenses to alter how light reaches your sensor. Filters allow for more technical flexibility. However, if used correctly, filters can add impressive creative characteristics.

ND - NEUTRAL DENSITY

Neutral density filters block a specific amount of light measured in stops. They allow you to use slower shutter speeds, wide-open apertures, or high ISO values without overexposing your images (page 53).

NC - NEUTRAL CLEAR

Neutral clear filters are primarily used for protective purposes on lenses (page 41). The UV version can also block ultraviolet light to help reduce blue coloring in your image seen at sea level or high altitudes.

PL - POLARIZER

Polarizing filters help reduce reflections and glare in your image. They can also enhance contrast and color saturation, especially in a blue sky. Polarizers generally aren't very useful, but they are fun and can be helpful in some circumstances.

IMPLEMENTING

Different types of filters are available, such as colored glass, mist, and optical effects. However, they usually aren't needed because of editing applications.

The only filter that genuinely has an enormous benefit is the ND filter. That is because ND blocks excessive light caused by creative exposure settings such as prolonged shutter speeds. The effect caused by an ND filter is impossible to recreate when editing (page 95).

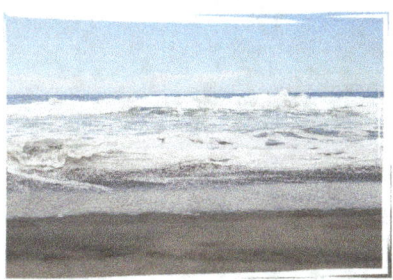

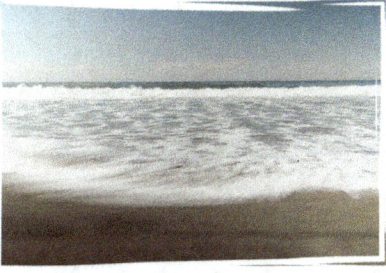

Normal fast-shutter
Exposing the image properly will sharply capture all of the motion.

Slow-shutter with ND
Using an ND allows you to soften the motion without overexposing the image.

Activity #17

Use a neutral density filter and practice taking pictures with a slow shutter speed during daylight hours. The best subject to try is flowing water.

5

Exposure

A core fundamental of photography is about finding the perfect balance of time, size, and sensitivity to capture beauty!

This process is called exposure and consists of:

- Shutter speed

- Aperture

- ISO

Shutter speed

Shutter speed allows you to capture photos using the factors of time and motion.

LIGHT CONTROL: TIME

You can adjust the shutter at different speeds. These speeds are the amount of time that light is exposed to the sensor. You can also select "bulb" to determine the exposure time based on how long you press the shutter release trigger.

Faster speed (e.g., 1/1,000 sec)—> **less light**

Slower speed (e.g., 1/15 sec)—> **more light**

CREATIVE CONTROL: MOTION

Once the shutter opens, all movements are captured on the sensor until it closes. Generally, it is best to capture sharp images handheld (page 49) by keeping the shutter speed at least the reciprocal of the focal length (e.g., an 85mm lens would be 1/85 sec). However, longer shutter speeds when stabilized with a tripod can be very useful to achieve a soft appearance.

Faster speed—> **less motion**

Slower speed—> **more motion**

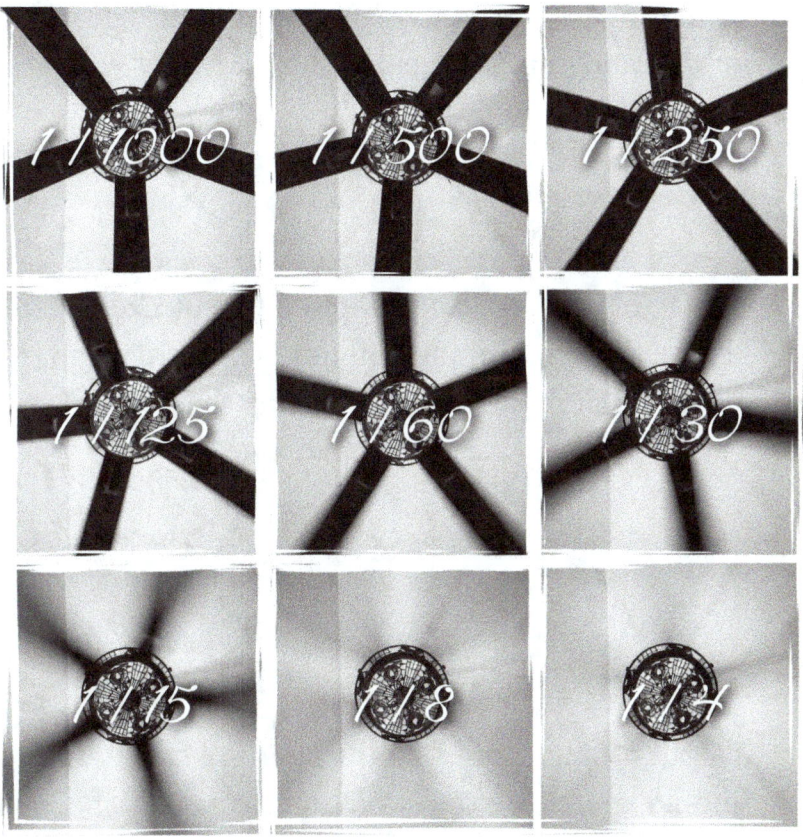

Activity #18

Take multiple pictures of various subjects at different shutter speeds using the "M" or "S"/"Tv" mode (page 21) on your camera. Review your pictures and reflect on what worked and what didn't.

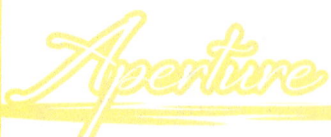

Aperture allows you to capture photos using the factors of size and depth of field.

LIGHT CONTROL: SIZE

You can adjust the aperture to different sizes. These sizes control the amount of light that can come through the lens before it reaches the sensor.

Smaller aperture (e.g., F/22) --> *less light*

Bigger aperture (e.g., F/2.8) --> *more light*

CREATIVE CONTROL: DEPTH OF FIELD

Depth of field caused by the aperture can control what should be in focus and what doesn't need to be in focus. Big apertures are commonly used with portraits to blur out the background for a dreamy look. Small apertures are often used with landscapes to achieve absolute sharpness in everything. It is up to you to determine what aperture to use as each one will significantly change the look of your image.

Smaller aperture --> *more depth*

Bigger aperture --> *less depth*

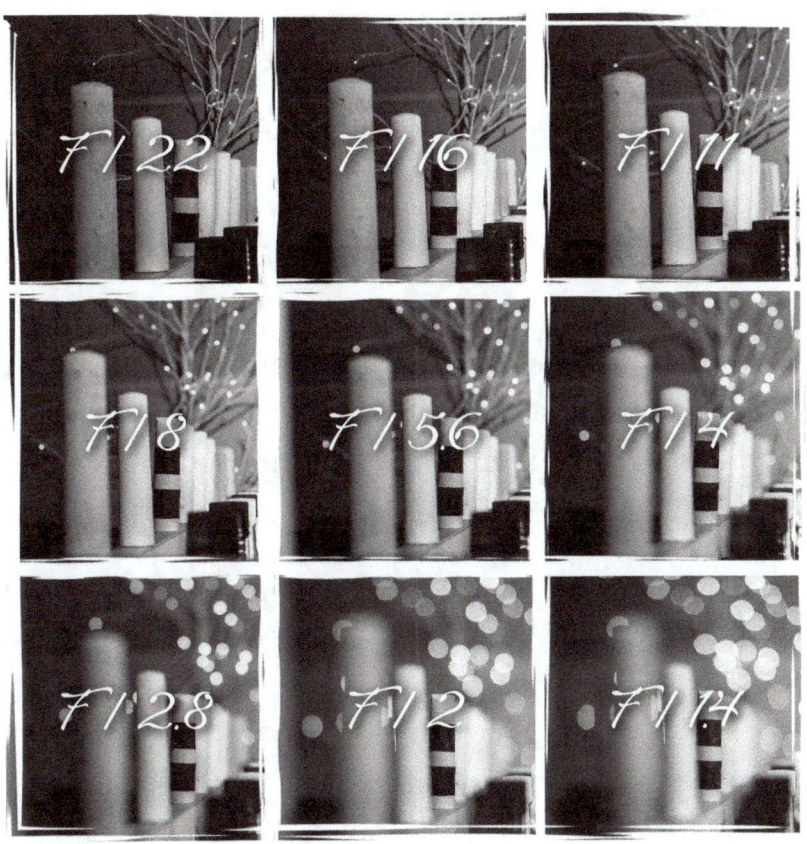

Activity #19

Take multiple pictures of various subjects at different apertures using the "M" or "A"/"Av" mode (page 21) on your camera. Review your pictures and reflect on what worked and what didn't.

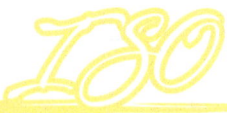

ISO allows you to capture photos using the factors of sensitivity and grain. Fun fact: ISO stands for "International Organization for Standardization."

LIGHT CONTROL: SENSITIVITY

The ISO is the last exposure control component. You can adjust it to control how sensitive the sensor should be to light (let in from the aperture and shutter speed).

Lower ISO (e.g., 100) → *less reactive to light*

Higher ISO (e.g., 6,400) → *more reactive to light*

CREATIVE CONTROL: GRAIN

The higher you bring up the ISO, the more noticeable the noise grain in your image becomes. You can use grain creatively, but it will often decrease sharpness by becoming more prominent than the textures in your image. For a clean image, keep the ISO at your camera's native level or below 640.

Lower ISO → *less grain*

Higher ISO → *more grain*

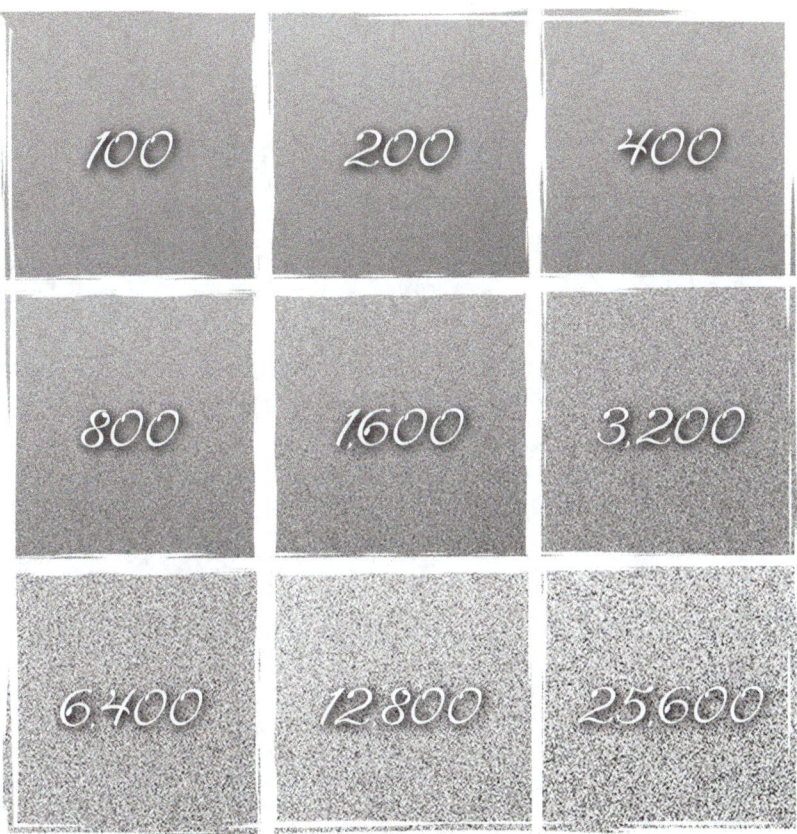

Activity #20

Take multiple pictures of various subjects at different ISO values using the "M" or "P" mode (page 21) on your camera. Review your pictures and reflect on what worked and what didn't.

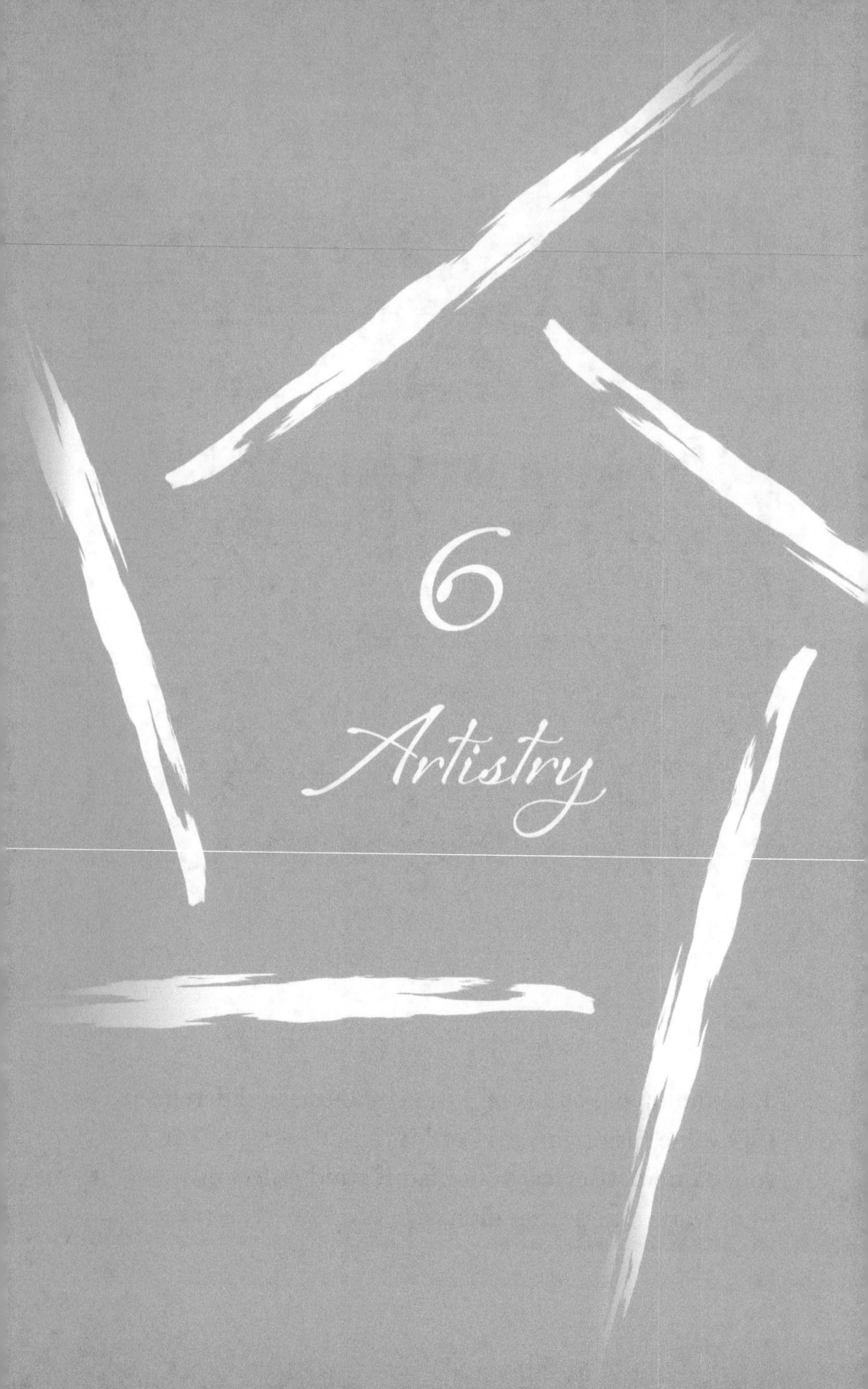

6

Artistry

Photography isn't just about what you can see, but also what you can't see!

You can make your images very artistic by utilizing:

- *Color psychology*

- *Black and white*

- *Focal lengths*

- *Color theory*

- *Philosophy*

- *Locations*

- *Lighting*

- *Posing*

- *Styles*

- *Flash*

Color psychology

Color consists much of the beauty in our photographs. However, they can be used strategically for aesthetics and to visually evoke a feeling.

INTERACTION

Everything we interact with has a color. It could just be a bland grey or a vibrant red. However, have you ever thought about how different colors can have a subliminal affect on you?

Utilize colors to your advantage. Use them in a way that helps tell stories in a much more powerful way in your photography.

ASSOCIATION

Every color is associated with something that we get a feeling from. The emotion can vary depending on where or how you use a color. Of course, this can only be partially accurate as the culture that you live in can significantly affect the way you perceive them.

For the large majority of cultures (especially in Western countries), the following chart is valid. Don't we all associate urgency with the color red? It is, after all, the color of a stop sign.

Orange: warm, happy, optimistic, and energetic.

Yellow: irritable, humorous, and fun.

Red: exciting, bold, urgent, and loving.

Green: healthy, growth, and acceptance.

Blue: cold, calm, trustworthy, and masculine.

Pink: soft, sweet, caring, and feminine.

Purple: mysterious, luxurious, and imaginative.

Brown: natural, earthy, and reliable.

Grey: sophisticated, dedicated, and classic.

Black: strong, powerful, and authoritative.

White: simple, clean, practical, and pure.

Activity #21

Create a few photos, each displaying different colors. Ask your friends and family what they think or feel about each picture.

Black and white

The majority of all photos are in full color. However, that does not mean black and white is a meaningless form of photography—quite the opposite. Black and white is very impactful, and you should utilize it.

COLOR VS MONOCHROMATIC

When you look at a monochromatic photo, you will pay more attention to the fine elements. These elements include shapes, textures, shading, and contrasts.

Full color is undeniably beautiful, but it can also be very distracting. Use the monochromatic color profile (page 39) if you intend to captivate the simplicity in a photograph by bringing attention to the fine elements.

CHOOSING YOUR IMAGES WISELY

Not all images should be monochromatic. There seems to be a common trend in our culture to take a boring photo, make it black and white, add a grain effect, and call it... ***artistic?*** That doesn't seem to be the purpose of black and white photography. Instead, it should concentrate on the simplicity concept that "less is more." Keep this in mind the next time you decide if you should process a photo to black and white, sepia, or cyanotype.

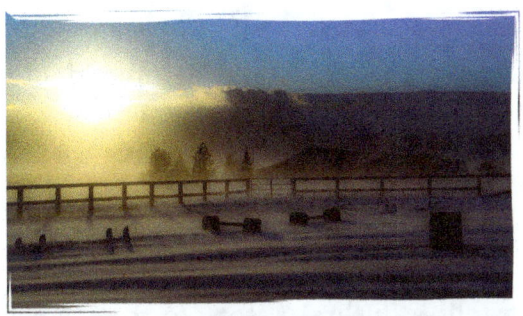

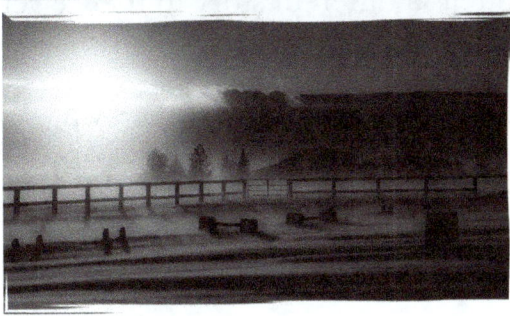

Examine each photo and compare what you pay attention to most. You may also use a piece of paper to cover the other image if that helps.

When looking at the top photo, notice how you pay attention to the distracting colors. There is much more beauty to this photo than just the colors.

Now, when you look at the bottom photo, notice how you pay more attention to the shapes, textures, shading, and contrasts. This example demonstrates how black and white photography can be beneficial!

Activity #22

Go through some of your pictures (or take new ones) and apply a black and white color profile. Do you like the color or the black and white version more?

Focal lengths

Using different focal lengths provides flexibility and perspective to your image because of its optical effect.

OPTICAL DISTANCE

Each focal length tells a different story to the viewer, and you can use them in any situation.

Wide (≤35mm) *- shows the environment*

Standard (~50mm) *- human eye equivalent*

Telephoto (≥70mm) *- isolates subjects*

DISTORTION AND COMPRESSION

The longer the focal length you use, the further away you must be from your subject. The optics compress what you see by making near and far objects closer together. The opposite is true if you use a shorter focal length, giving you a distorted look.

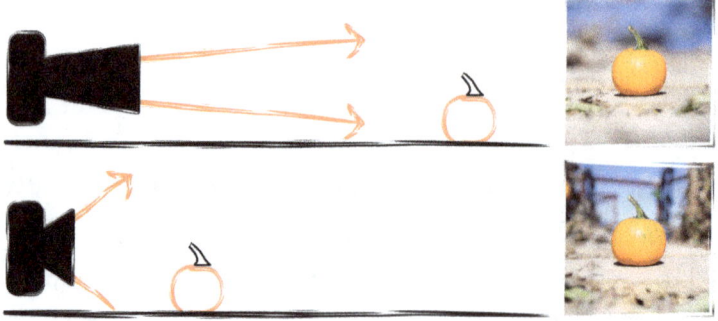

FIELD OF VIEW

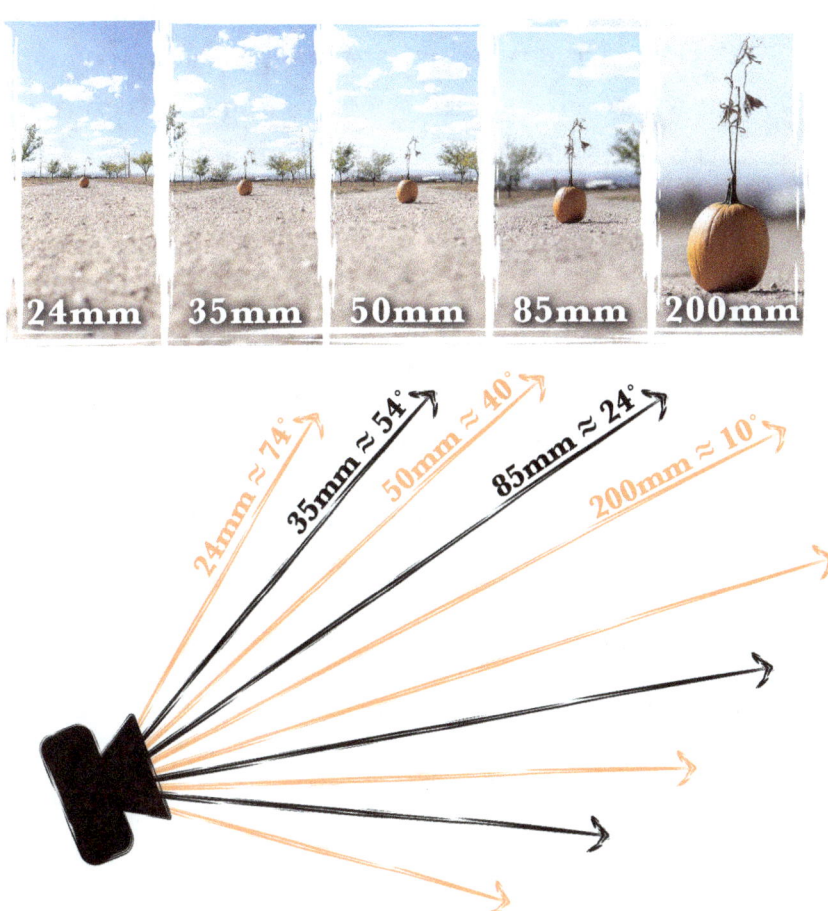

Activity #23

Take multiple pictures of the same object, each with a different focal length. Once finished, compare the results, think about what makes each photo unique, and select the one you like most!

Color theory

There are primary colors that all colors are made from. Mix two of them, and you receive a secondary color. Mix one primary color with one secondary color, and you will receive a tertiary color. You can keep repeating this process to get any color imaginable.

ADDITIVE (RGB)

RGB is for electronic applications such as lights and sensors. When colors mix, they become brighter.

Key: *white is the <u>combination</u> of all colors.*

Primary: *red, green, blue.*

Secondary: *magenta, yellow, cyan.*

Tertiary: *rose, orange, lime, mint, azure, violet.*

SUBTRACTIVE (CMYK)

CMYK is for physical applications such as painting and printing. When colors mix, they become darker.

Key: *white is the <u>absence</u> of all colors.*

Primary: *cyan, magenta, yellow, black.*

Secondary: *blue, red, green.*

Tertiary: *azure, violet, rose, orange, lime, mint.*

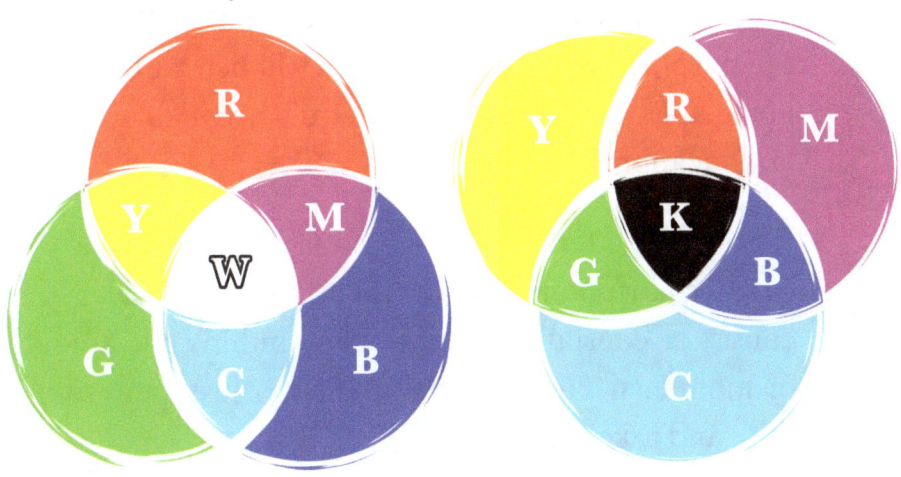

RGB System:

CMYK System:

Color harmony

You can use a color palette with harmony rules to help you create and edit pictures.

Monochromatic: *different shades of one color*

Complimentary: *opposite colors* (e.g., red & cyan)

Analogous: *a set of multiple similar colors*

Triad: *three completely distinct colors*

(e.g., orange & violet & mint)

Activity #24

Take and edit a series of pictures demonstrating each harmony rule listed above. What was your favorite?

Philosophy

The problem with photography is that we tend to create images with no real impact (page 9). By learning the purpose of photography, you will benefit from being able to create something truly original, authentic, and meaningful.

It doesn't matter if you are a professional or just a casual smartphone photographer. All of our lives consist of constantly capturing an unthinkable amount of moments. However, have you ever just spent some time and asked why?

PURPOSE OF PHOTOGRAPHY

Photography is a type of communication media that is about capturing light. It comes from two Greek words that translate to "painting with light."

Essentially, light contains the power for us to:

+ ***Preserve moments***
+ ***Express emotion***
+ ***Capture beauty***
+ ***Tell a story***

All of that is energy. You can photographically paint with it to convey a visual message about who we are!

We take pictures because we can bridge
the art of light with humanity.

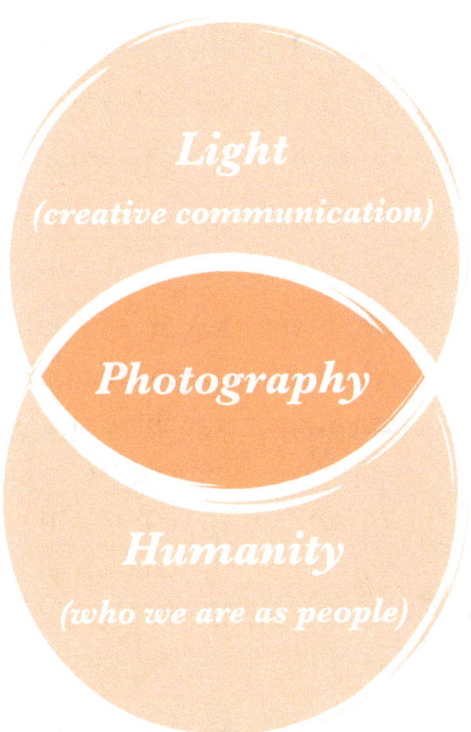

*When you begin to
look at photography
from this perspective,
you realize the
importance this art
form has and the
opportunities that you
can do with it!*

Activity #25

Based on the philosophy described in this spread,
write down what photography means to you. You
may not think of it immediately, so spend as much
time as you like. Doing this will help you create
influential photos with a visual message!

Locations

We often love to take pictures because we are amazed at where we are. It could be a sunset, interesting urban art, or a majestic mountain range. Regardless, wouldn't you agree that the location is essential for a great picture?

JUSTIFYING A LOCATION

Many people say that an image cannot justify the beauty of a location. To create a photo that justifies a location, you need to imagine exactly how you will photograph it. Just aiming your camera and clicking a button will not work. It would help to put in the effort and thoroughly think about how the picture will be the best possible. Always be challenging yourself to innovate your craft (page 13).

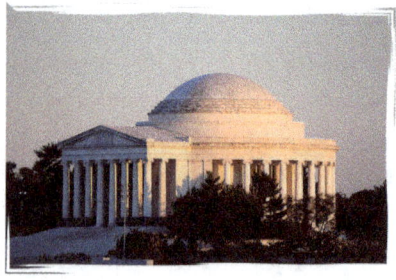 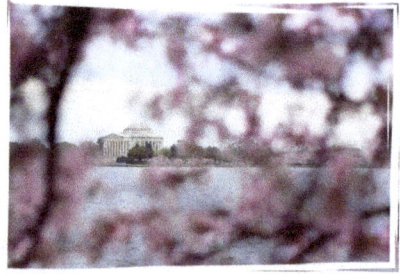

FIRST ATTEMPT   **SECOND ATTEMPT**

Sometimes, you may think that you already captured a good picture. However, by revisiting, you can approach the location differently to get a better picture.

CHOOSING A GREAT SPOT

The first step once you have arrived at a location, is to find a spot. Where you decide to take a picture may be the difference between a good and great photo. Many factors (among all the topics in this book) help you decide on a spot.

Make sure to immerse yourself in the location and scout for spots to get the best pictures. When choosing a spot, make sure you consider:

1: *Quality, direction, and color of the light*

2: *Elements to compose the image uniquely*

3: *Contains what you want to capture*

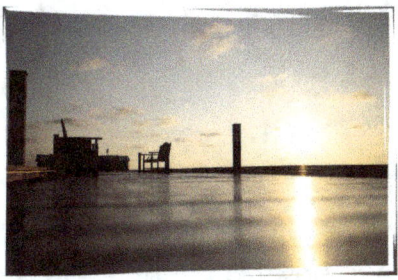

Example:
1: soft, direct, and golden
2: reflective pier
3: sunrise

Activity #26

Go to a park and challenge yourself to find the perfect spot. Think about finding the perfect picture spot as a hidden treasure. It may be obscure.

Lighting

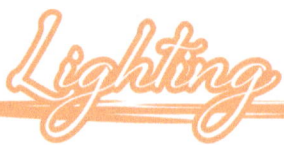

The way you understand and use light in your craft may be one of the most powerful skills to have.

QUALITY OF LIGHT

Naturally, light is initially hard, causing the shadows to have a sharp edge. However, when hard light is diffused, it becomes soft. You can capture diffused light when it bounces off a non-glossy surface or passes through something translucent (like a cloud). Hard and soft light have different advantages, but it ultimately depends on what you want in your photo.

Hard lighting

Soft lighting

DIRECTION OF LIGHT

The direction of light you choose will depend on the look you want in your photo. To achieve this, pay attention to your position relative to the shadows.

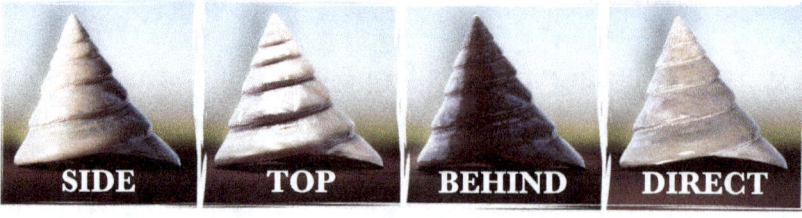

SIDE   TOP   BEHIND   DIRECT

Color of light

In color theory (page 69), you can mix colors to create other colors. However, the natural color of light is usually white (5,600K) and only changes color based on when it interacts with something.

For example, when the light reflects off grass, it will change to a greenish color. Or if you have light shining through a red gel, it will change to a reddish color.

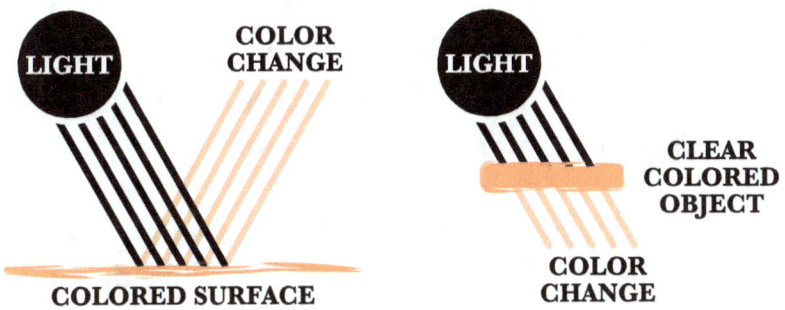

Activity #27

Go to an area with many trees or buildings on a sunny day. Bring your camera and notice how the quality, direction, and color of light affect each picture you take. Think about what worked, what didn't, and what you could do differently.

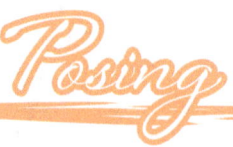

Posing

The body language tells us a lot about people. When capturing a portrait, we aim to make our subjects look as best as possible. That all starts with how we communicate with them.

INTENTION

Everyone has different expectations when being photographed, and it is important to understand them.

Females - when taking pictures of a woman, she should look pretty. Pose in a way that makes her look thin while enhancing her curves to form an hourglass body shape figure.

Males - when taking pictures of a man, he should look cool. Pose him to appear confident while defining an upside-down trapezoid body shape figure.

DIRECTING

Capturing someone's beauty is not only limited to their physical appearance. Their emotion and personality are equally worth capturing (page 117). Getting your subject to laugh and move can help with this. Especially considering that a pose held over a few seconds will appear fake.

STANDARDS

Regardless of the pose, there are simple standards that should be used to avoid unpleasing looks.

Head - avoid a double chin and keep the camera perspective preferably at eye level (page 87).

Body - capturing the body at an angle away from the camera's direct view is preferred. A 45° angle is best.

Arms/hands - the arms and hands can be used as leading lines for composition (page 89). Keeping a gap between the body and arms, and bending them to avoid a straight or right angle (90°) is also attractive.

Legs/feet - keep the body weight on one foot, slightly bending one knee. This creates a contrapposto figure.

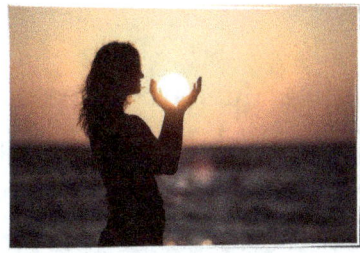

Always find innovative ways to create exciting and unusual pictures (page 9).

Activity #28

Practice with a friend or family member. Pose them to appear looking their best. If you feel that you have succeeded, capture a portrait of it.

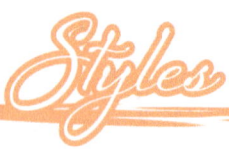
Styles

Your photographic signature is the unique way you take pictures and is known as your style. How you develop a style is based on your experience, genre, and approach.

EXPERIENCE

You will not know what your style is immediately. It takes lots of time and experimentation before you understand what it is. A process that requires you to explore everything about taking pictures. You might think it is one style and soon discover it is something else. With lots of experience, you will naturally find your style.

GENRE

The genre may be the least impactful part of your style but is nonetheless a significant contributor. Knowing what you most enjoy taking pictures of should make it easier to develop a style. You can categorize what you like taking pictures of, such as artificial, natural, or people (page 111). You could include subcategories such as events, birds, portraits, flowers, travel, or food.

Photographers often confuse trends with styles, but each is entirely different. Trends can be fun, but have little to do with styles.

APPROACH

Determining how you will take a picture significantly contributes to your style. For example, if you bring one hundred photographers to a park, each one will approach it differently. Your approach consists of your observation and then your response to that observation.

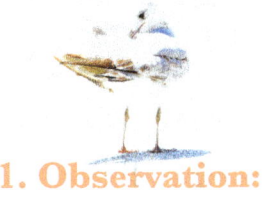

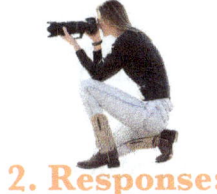

1. Observation:

paying attention to your surroundings and understanding how the world works allows you to see things uniquely.

2. Response:

based on the observation, you will determine how to create the picture using the elements and your camera.

Activity #29

Go for a walk somewhere without your camera. Stop at areas that fascinate you and try to determine how you would capture a photo there. If you feel inspired enough, go back to get your camera to capture it!

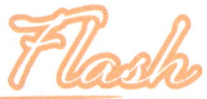

Flash

When there isn't enough light to capture a scene with an average shutter speed, artificial light, such as a flash unit, can be extremely useful.

FLASH MODES

Choose a flash mode depending on your approach.

TTL - automatic mode that uses "through-the-lens" metering. TTL is the least complicated mode to use but may produce undesirable or inconsistent results.

Manual - you can fire manually by selecting the power measured in fractions. It allows for the most control, but failure to set it correctly will ruin your picture.

FLASH SETUPS

Choose a flash setup depending on the circumstances.

Camera flash - you can use the built-in flash, but it is better to attach a flash unit in the hot shoe of your camera for greater control.

Off-camera flash (OCF) - you can use a radio, cord, or infrared trigger to fire multiple flash units remotely. OCF requires the most setup time but will allow you to have significant control over the lighting.

Flash techniques

Every photo will require a different flash technique to achieve your desired lighting look based on quality, direction, and color (page 75).

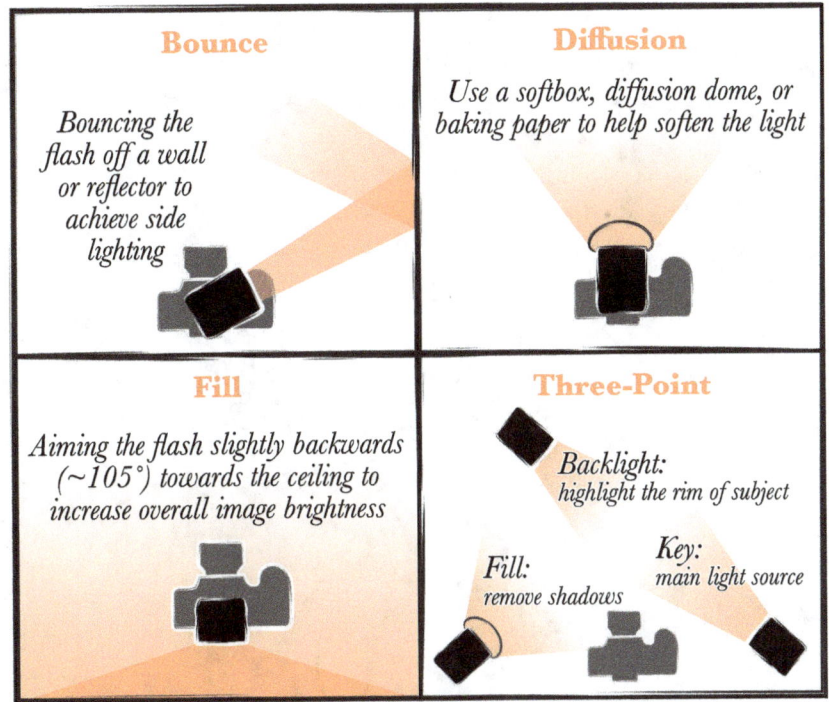

Bounce	Diffusion
Bouncing the flash off a wall or reflector to achieve side lighting	*Use a softbox, diffusion dome, or baking paper to help soften the light*
Fill	**Three-Point**
Aiming the flash slightly backwards (~105°) towards the ceiling to increase overall image brightness	*Backlight: highlight the rim of subject* / *Fill: remove shadows* / *Key: main light source*

Activity #30

Use a flash unit on a still-life subject or your pet. Experiment with different modes, setups, and techniques to determine what works best for you.

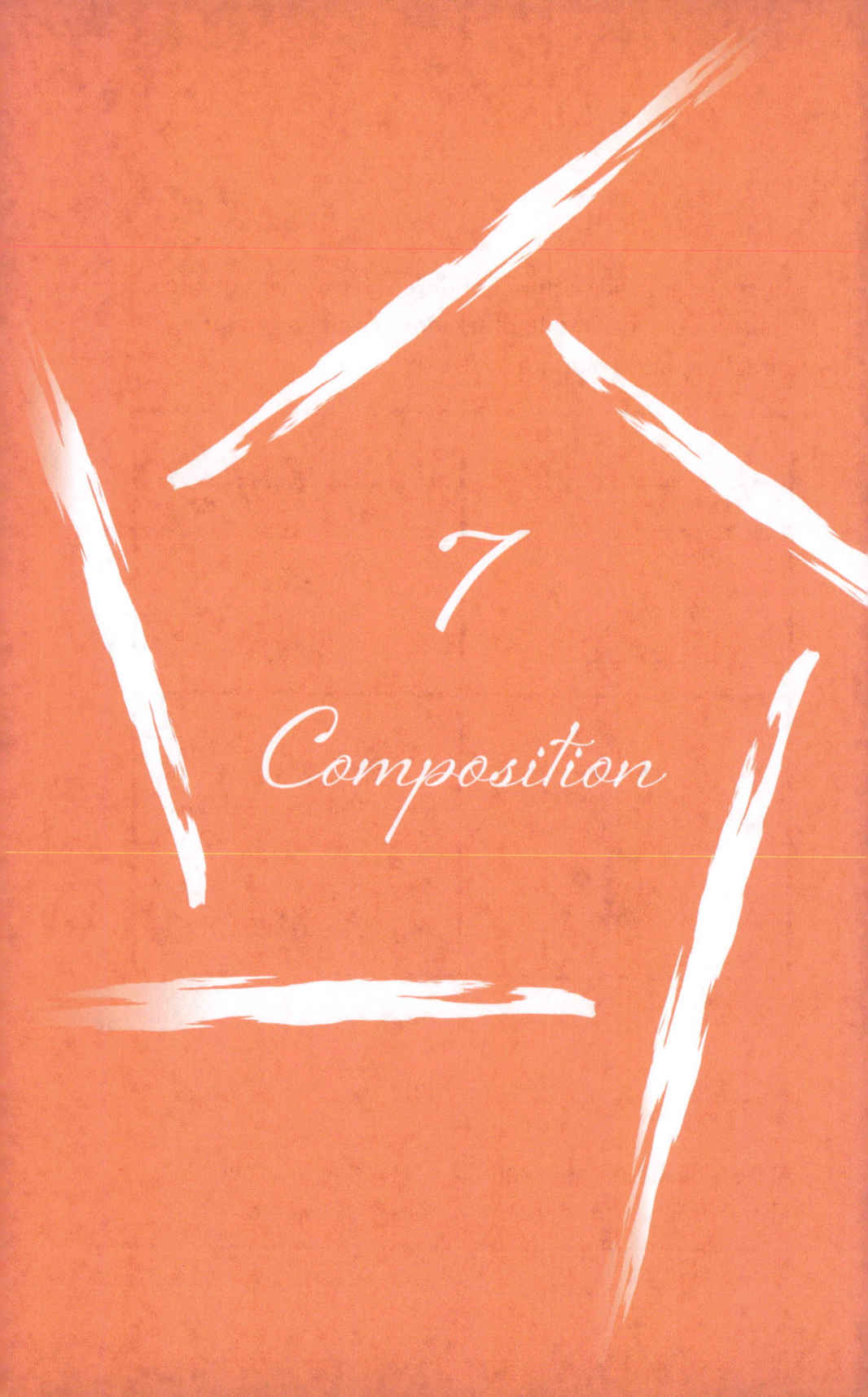

7

Composition

The composition in your photo is like architecture for a building. The beauty is what attracts people to enter, but the true importance is what you find inside

Discover how to compose your pictures by understanding:

- *Relationship*

- *Perspective*

- *Direction*

- *Aesthetic*

- *Balance*

Relationship

The most fundamental part of composition is placing the background, foreground, and subject. The relationship between these portions of composition lets you emphasize the energy you capture (page 71).

SIMPLE COMPOSITION

Composing for simplicity is using a few elements emphasizing only one type of energy.

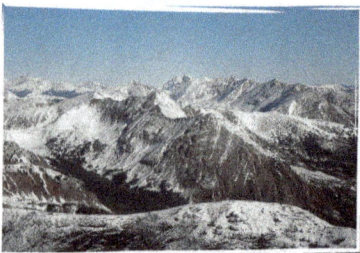

Using a limited number of composition elements will make the entire image become one coherent subject.

DYNAMIC COMPOSITION

Composing dynamically is often more difficult as you have several elements in the photograph to emphasize multiple forms of energy.

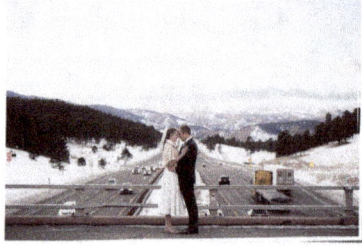

Using many composition elements will make every part of the image fit together seamlessly like a puzzle piece.

HARMONY ZONES

Think of harmony zones as a getting to know the image. Using the "Rule of Thirds" (roughly zone 3) is generally recommended because it isn't a direct connection (you need to get to know the photo first). However, there is no right or wrong option. It all depends on how you want your subject to appear.

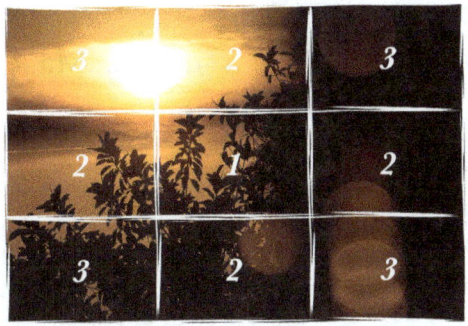

Zone 1: ***strong connection*** *(direct)*

Zone 2: ***moderate connection*** *(indirect)*

Zone 3: ***subtle connection*** *(pleasing)*

Activity #31

Experiment by capturing photos with simple and dynamic composition. Also, compose your pictures with the subject in different zones to discover how they can influence your work.

Perspective

The perspective you choose when creating a photograph is unique. Capturing an image with your own perspective is powerful because it allows others to see the way you visualize the world.

VARIETY

It is often a lazy and cliché approach to only photograph directly at a subject. Make sure you explore all the different angles to find the best one for the type of picture you want to capture.

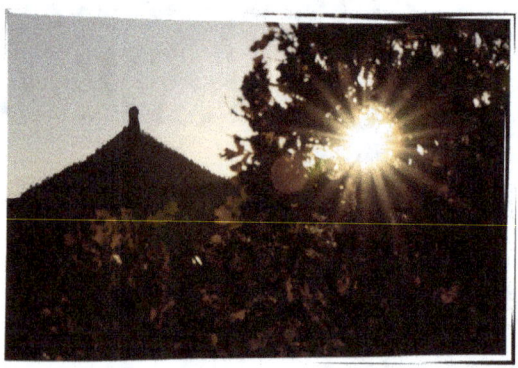

Finding an exciting or uncommon angle can add creativity and freshness to your photos. Doing this allows you and others to see the world in a novel way. Keeping a variety of perspectives in mind is a way to avoid capturing the same boring picture that everyone else photographs. There is always more to a scene than what you initially see.

ANGLE PSYCHOLOGY

How you look at something can have a subliminal affect on how you think about the subject.

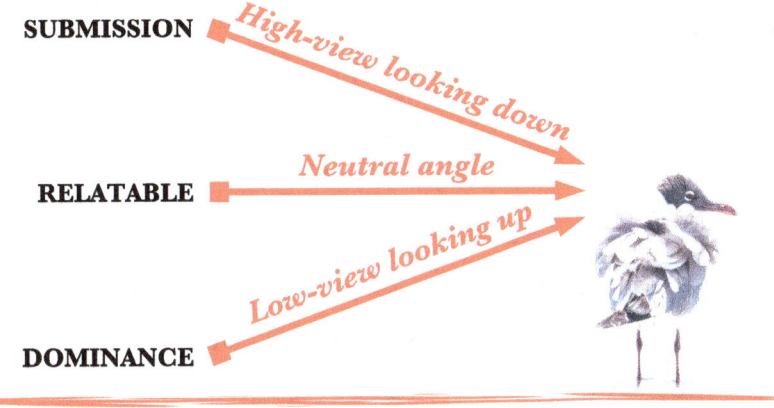

By choosing a perspective angle, you can convey a feeling to the image viewers. A neutral angle is excellent for simply capturing the subject. However, if you want the subject to appear more substantial than the viewers, angle the camera upwards. The opposite is also true if you capture the subject with the camera angle downwards.

Activity #32

Capture interesting angles of basic subjects. Do this by utilizing the elements around you, different lighting conditions, the environment, and depth of field.

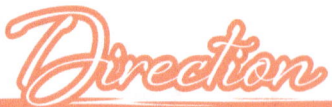
Direction

When walking, we follow the best path from what we observe. So, when you are composing a photo, think about the path your eyes are going to follow. It could be repetitive objects that eventually end up to a point of interest or many high-contrast lines that lead to your primary subject.

REPETITION

Look for objects that repeat themselves, such as a fence or a line of trees. Photographing these repeating objects allows the eyes to move seamlessly with them.

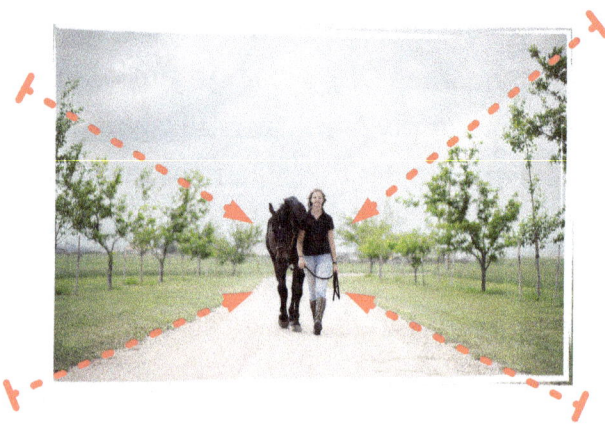

Repetition helps direct the eye to the critical parts of the frame. It also makes the image more interesting. Notice how the road and the repeating trees allow the eye to look at the girl with her horse immediately? That is the beauty of repetition.

LEADING LINES

Lines and edges are much more common than repetition. They can also make a more significant impact on your image viewers if used correctly.

When you look around, you will notice visual lines created from geometry and color. You can use those as leading lines. The purpose is to visually frame your image and to direct the eye to other parts of the image.

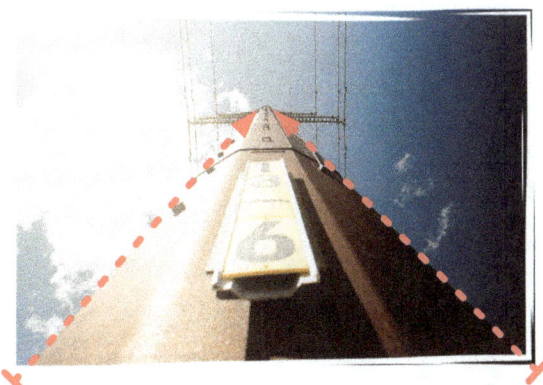

Look at the above photo. Notice how you initially looked at the sign, then to the top of the pole, then the sky? That is the beauty of leading lines.

Activity #33

Go to a park or walk around your living space. Compose each of your photos by utilizing any repeating objects or leading lines.

Aesthetic

To be creative with your composition, utilize the elements around you. Although not nearly the most crucial part of composition, this will allow you to increase the aesthetic appeal of your photographs.

PATTERNS

By noticing consistent patterns and symmetry, you can use them to add interest to your images.

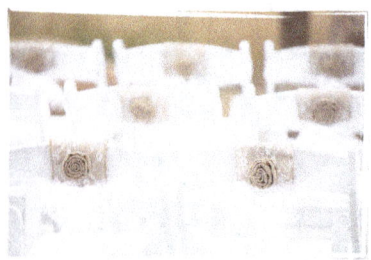

You can photograph these patterns or use them to complement another element in your picture.

SHAPES

Among everything, we see shapes: squares, triangles, circles, lines, and more. We see these in nature, in artificial things, and through our imagination.

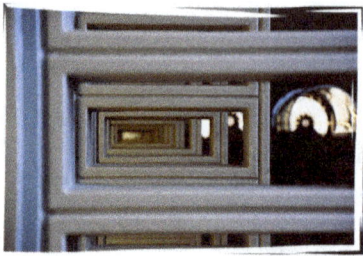

You can use these shapes creatively to compose your picture by uniquely framing the scene.

SPACE

What you choose to include or not to have in your images is a powerful decision. Space is an aesthetic element, but if used correctly, it can influence the story and bring a more significant emphasis to a subject.

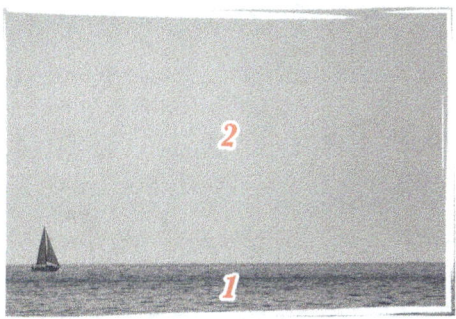

Positive space *(1)* - is the language you notice in a scene. It is how the viewer can understand and connect with your image.

Negative space *(2)* - is the emptiness that adds definition, value, and attraction to positive space. Without it, positive space has no purpose. The more you have of it, the more powerful it can become.

Activity #34

Go for a walk down a street and look for patterns, shapes, and negative space. Discover unique ways you can take pictures by utilizing these aesthetic elements.

Balance

Compositional balance allows you to express a feeling with your photograph. Keeping your picture balanced will convey a pleasant feeling, while an unbalanced picture may add tension. Both options are equally impactful, but you must determine the best approach for your photograph.

HORIZON

Keeping the horizon level is standard for a balanced image. This technique is especially beneficial for landscape photography. To help achieve this, you can use the straightening tool when editing (page 105).

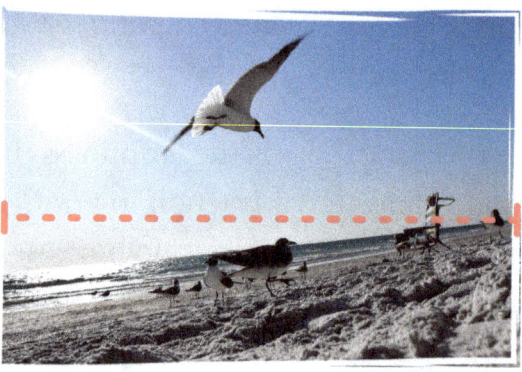

In some circumstances, keeping your horizon unleveled may be used to evoke an uncomfortable, exciting, or fantasy-like feeling. It is known as the "dutch-tilt" and is a common technique.

VISUAL WEIGHT

Your horizon may be perfectly level, but your image will still feel unbalanced if your visual weight is mostly on one side of the image.

Different parts of your image will contain visual weight and include details that demand attention from the eye. Think of high-contrast points, noticeable shapes, subjects, and out-of-place objects.

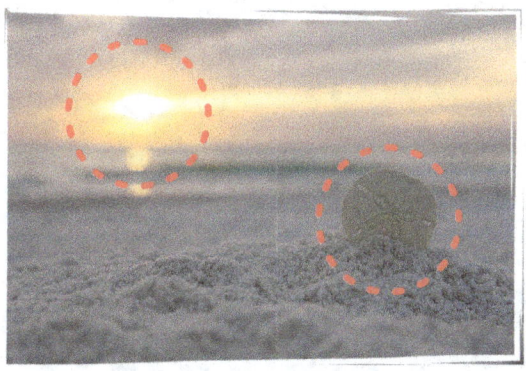

In the above image, the sand dollar and the sunset keep the photo balanced. It also utilizes the "Rule of Thirds" for good harmony (page 85).

Activity #35

Capture landscape photographs to keep them as balanced as possible. Keep the horizon level and place visual weight evenly.

8

Editing

Editing a picture is an essential step to achieve a polished look.

Enhance your pictures through the process of:

- *Color adjustments*

- *Tone adjustments*

- *Corrections*

- *Retouching*

- *Cropping*

- *Workflow*

- *Sharing*

Color adjustments

Adjusting the colors of your pictures is a great way to add quality to them. However, you must be careful because altering or enhancing the colors too much may make your pictures look unnatural. Before making any adjustments, make sure you have read color psychology (page 63) and theory (page 69).

Hue

When wanting to change a color, you can alter the hue. This tool will reclassify a color to one that is similar.

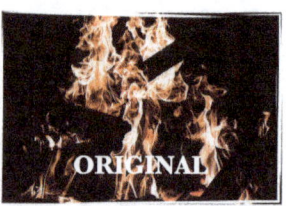 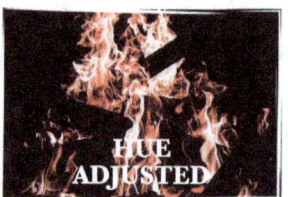

Saturation

Saturation is a handy tool to make your images more attractive. It doesn't necessarily add more color but rather intensifies the colors.

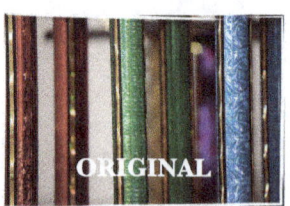 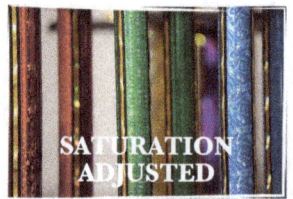

Color luminance

Colors also have brightness. You can increase or decrease the brightness of a specific color to make it more noticeable.

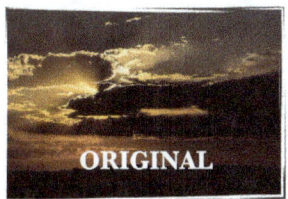 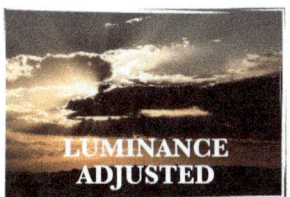

Color grading

You can add a color cast to the shadows, midtones, and highlights of the tonal range (page 99). Color grading is an often utilized method in cinema post-production to help achieve a specific feeling and look to a movie.

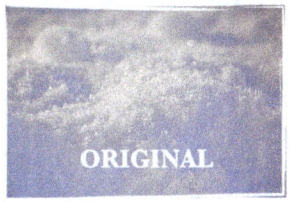 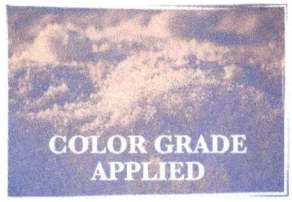

Activity #36

Search your library and find pictures to experiment with editing. Have fun and discover unique ways to alter or enhance the colors of your images creatively.

Tone adjustments

The tonal range consists of darkness, brightness, and everything in between. Display a more outstanding visual impression by editing the tonal range of all your images.

MAIN SETTINGS

Each editing application differs, but these are the main tone adjustment settings.

— **Blacks:** *absolute darkness (no details seen)*

— **Shadows:** *darkness with details visible*

● **Midtones:** *optimal balance of tones*

✛ **Highlights:** *brightness with details visible*

✛ **Whites:** *absolute brightness (no details seen)*

EXPOSURE HARMONY

It is a challenge to find a good balance of the tonal range that is creative and accurate. You can learn what each tone setting does, but only experience will give you a good understanding. Editing is a very interactive process, so experiment when adjusting your photos to see what works best.

HISTOGRAM

To achieve the best tones, have your histogram display a pyramid-like shape across the entire range. However, that isn't always possible if you want a creative yet natural-looking photograph.

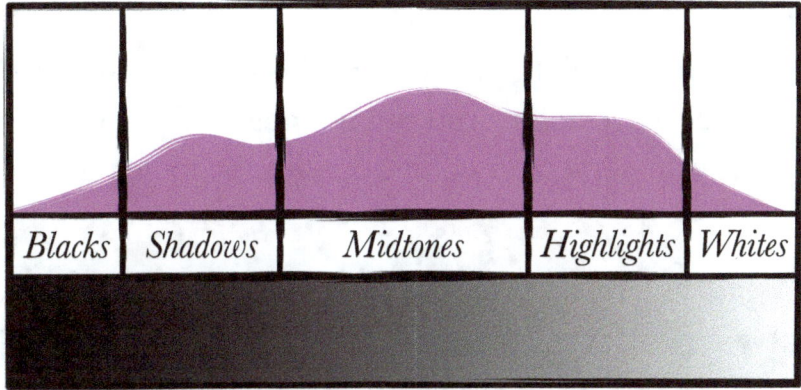

| Blacks | Shadows | Midtones | Highlights | Whites |

CONTRAST

Contrast adjustments will make the tones look less or more visually noticeable in your image. By carefully utilizing the contrast tool, you can make your images look exciting. Just be careful not to exaggerate it.

Activity #37

Take some sunset/sunrise pictures in **RAW** (if possible) and edit your favorite ones by experimenting with tone adjustment tools in your editing software.

Corrections

Your camera and lens will sometimes produce undesirable images due to a technical fault. To fix these problems, you can use correction tools.

Noise corrections

Shoot at a higher ISO (page 59), and your image will likely have noise. You can use noise reduction features in your camera or editing application to help with this.

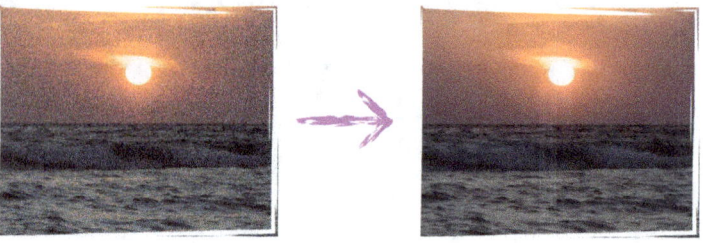

Color corrections

Shooting in a RAW file format (page 43) will permit you to make precise color corrections when editing your images. Correct your image by adjusting colors (page 97) and white balance (page 37).

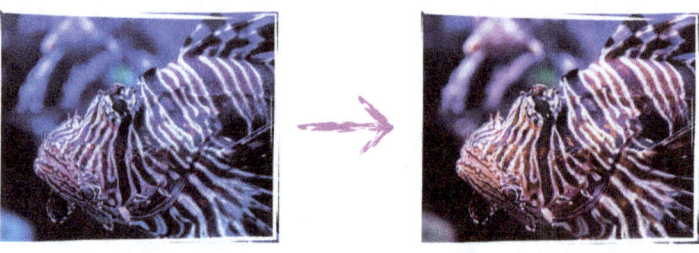

LENS CORRECTIONS

Most lenses will produce distortion, vignette, or chromatic aberration. These are usually not wanted in your images, but you can fix them using an editing application. The only lens error you cannot correct is focus blur (unless you use an AI editing feature).

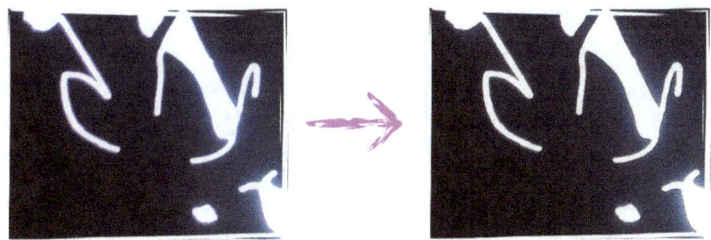

CORRECTING CHROMATIC ABERRATION

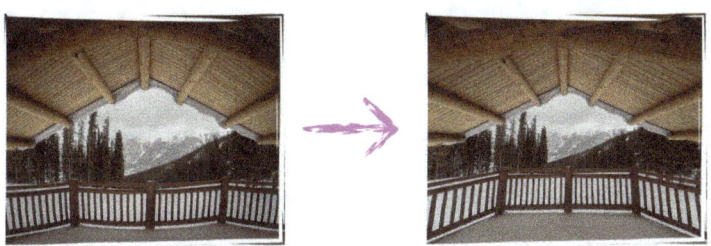

CORRECTING DISTORTION AND VIGNETTE

Activity #38

Find images in your photo library that you could correct. Using your editing application, experiment with the different features to fix noise, color, distortion, vignette, or chromatic aberration.

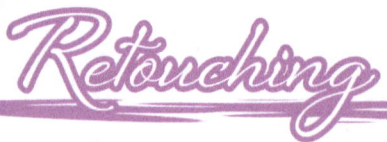

Retouching

We often take pictures with elements we wish would've been different. By using retouching tools, you can perfect your pictures by changing or removing unpleasant elements.

HEALING

It is possible to remove elements in your photo, such as distracting objects in the background. Your editing application can do this by copying different parts of your image and pasting it over the objects you want to remove or modify.

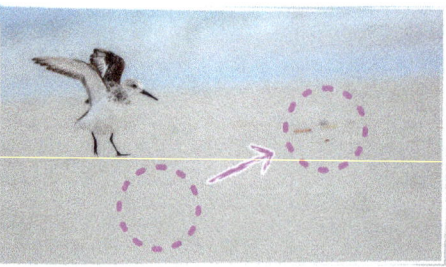

HEALING PROCESS

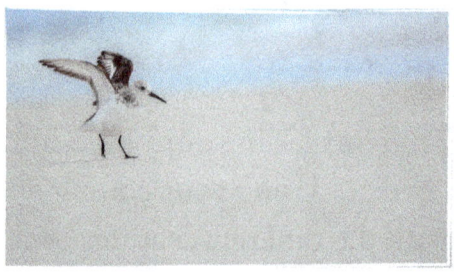

HEALING COMPLETE

103

Masking

When editing pictures, your main settings will affect the entire image. However, when using a masking tool, you can adjust the settings for only a selected part of your picture. Masking allows you to adjust the white balance (page 37) and the tonal range (page 99) separately for each image element. Doing this helps create a more dynamic and creative photo.

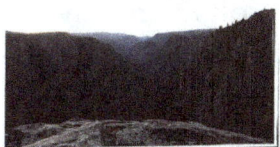

WITHOUT MASK

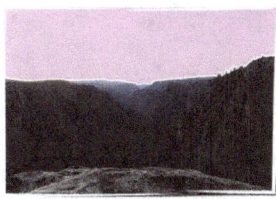

ADDING THE MASK

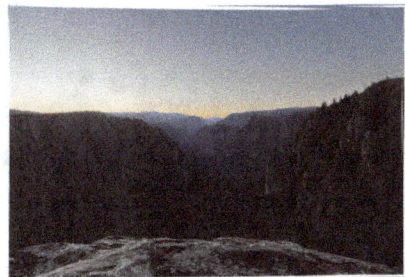

MASK SETTINGS APPLIED

Activity #39

Use your editing application to edit a few pictures. Try to utilize the retouching tools of healing and masking. How can you improve the appearance of your pictures without making them look fake?

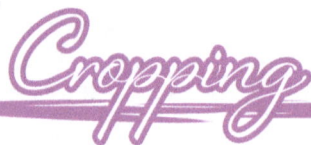
Cropping

Being able to crop provides an opportunity to improve the composition of your photographs (page 83). Cropping helps tell the story and evoke a feeling.

BENEFITS OF CROPPING

The beauty of cropping is that it allows you to change the photo in a big way after you've captured it. Here are two significant ways you can improve a photo by cropping. Your editing application might have a crop overlay tool to help with this process.

Isolate - you can crop out distracting objects in a photo or keep the photo more balanced by only showing part of the image.

Reinforce - you can improve the composition by cropping the image in unique ways that direct the eye differently compared to the original photo.

STRAIGHTENING

We often take pictures at an angle that usually appears unbalanced to the eye (page 93). Especially when taking pictures of landscapes, it is essential to keep the horizon leveled. Most editing applications allow you to crop by rotating the image to fix this issue.

Aspect ratios

Ratios are based on the relationship between the vertical length and the horizontal length. You can use each aspect ratio to compose your pictures differently and to display your images in unique ways.

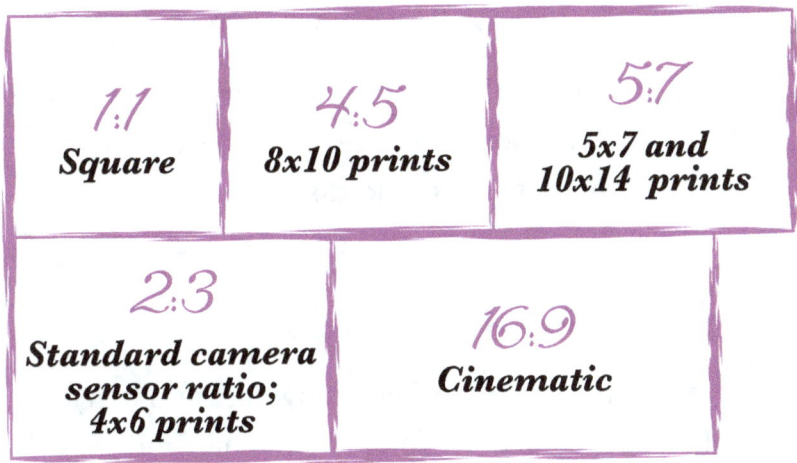

Choose an aspect ratio that works best with your style (page 79) and the type of pictures you captured.

Activity #40

Take various pictures and try to crop them in as many ways as possible. The goal is to achieve the most fascinating appearance. Once done, export each version and compare them all.

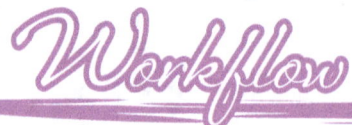

Your photography workflow is how you handle data. From the moment you take a picture to when you archive it in permanent storage. Someone could argue that this is the most integral part of photography.

IMPORTING AND CULLING

As soon as possible, insert your memory card into your computer and begin importing. If necessary, select the ones you want to keep and discard.

ORGANIZING AND EDITING

Keep your pictures in folders by date and place them in collections by activity (page 11). This practice will help prevent you from losing pictures. When you finish organizing, get creative and edit your favorites!

STORAGE AND BACKUP

Keep multiple copies of your pictures on at least two separate storage devices. Consider keeping one away from your residence or in a fireproof safe. Once your pictures are safely stored and backed up, you can delete them from your memory cards (page 35).

Equipment:
Prepare all of
your gear so it
is ready to go
(page 123).

Adventure:
Go have some
fun and take
lots of pretty
pictures!

Computer:
Import to your
photo library
and organize
them.

Sharing:
Export your
photos and
share them
(page 109).

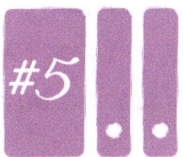

Backup:
Frequently
backup your
photos to a
separate device.

Activity #41

Draw and write out your workflow of how you will
handle your image data. The purpose of this is to
help you save time and storage space and, most
importantly, to prevent data loss.

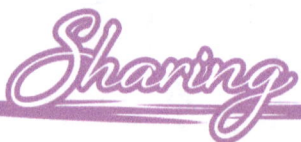

Sharing

There is no right or wrong way to enjoy your pictures. You could keep the pictures to yourself, or you could share them with the world.

EXPORTING YOUR IMAGES

Before sharing your pictures, you will need to export them from your editing application. Generally, the best file formats (page 43) for sharing are JPEG and PNG. The best export compression percentage is about 80%, which is a good balance of file size and quality.

SOCIAL MEDIA

Social media can be a great way to get attention for your work. However, you must be careful, as the amount of attention you get from social media does not reflect your ability to capture quality photos.

WEBSITE

Putting together a portfolio is a great way to share your best work. You can find many freemium and premium website hosting services available to accomplish this. When putting together a website, keep simplicity and ease of use in mind.

PRINTING

It is said that your pictures don't become true photographs until you print them. There is something extraordinary about seeing and feeling a printed image.

Before printing, make sure you calibrate your computer monitor. If ordering from a print lab, you can also pay extra to have them color-check your pictures. Color calibrating ensures that the pictures you see on your monitor look the same when printed.

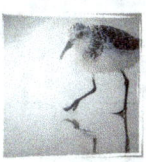 **Metallic** - a highly reflective finish and is excellent for images that have a more dramatic appearance.

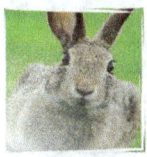 **Lustre** - a hybrid between metallic and matte finish. Lustre is a good option for all types of photos.

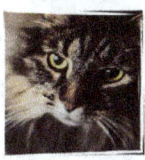 **Matte** - a low-reflective finish and is excellent for images that have a softer appearance.

Activity #42

Select a few images to export from your editing application. Share these images via website, social media, or print them.

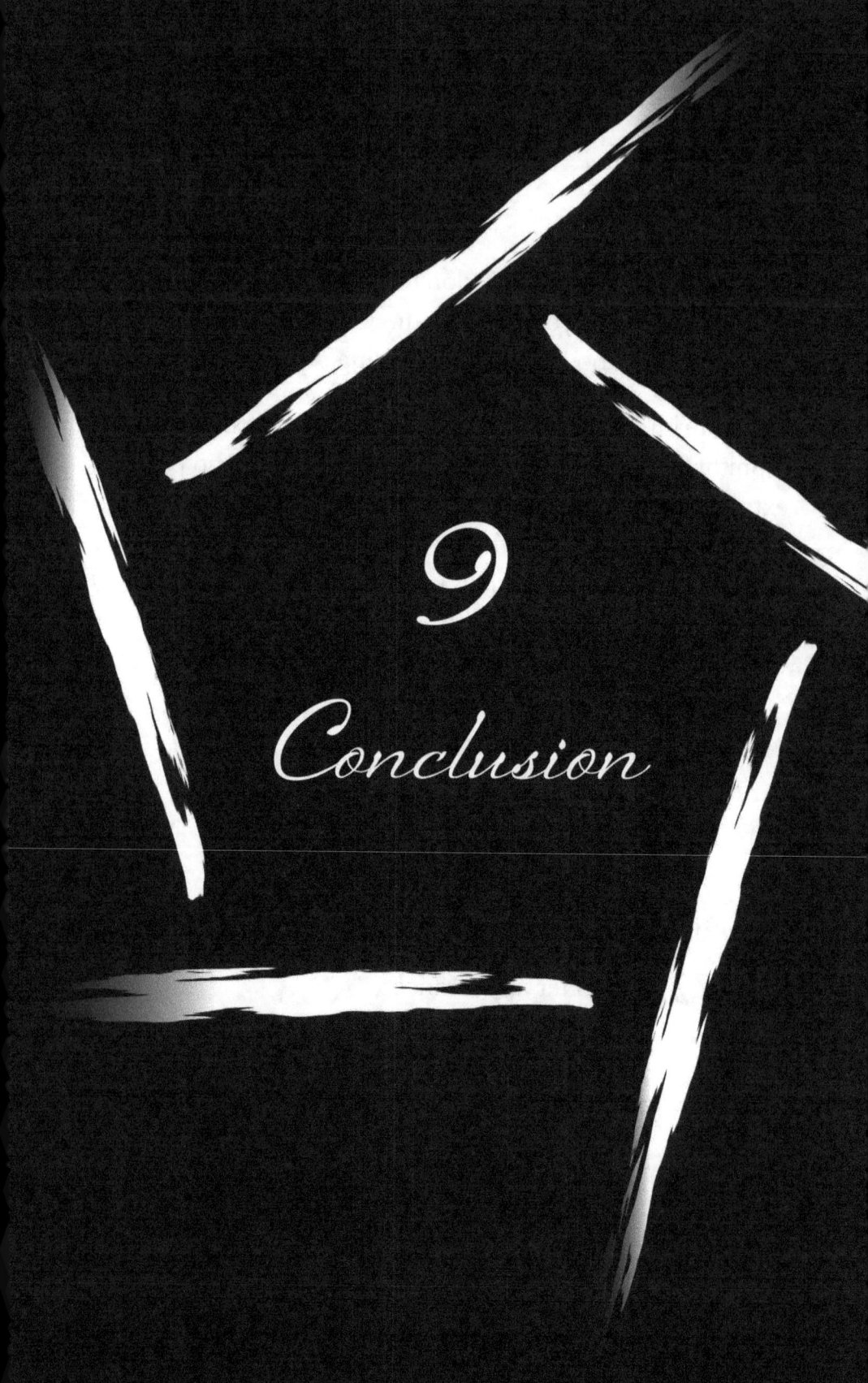

9

Conclusion

Your technique and approach to capturing photos may depend on your chosen genre interest.

In the final section of this book, explore how to capture subjects that are:

- *Artificial*

- *Natural*

- *People*

Also, check out the Appendix, Acknowledgments, and About the author.

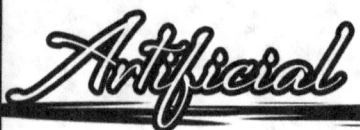

If there is anything we as people know how to do, it is the ability to create. We create words, experiences, habits, and most obviously, physical things.

Genres

All things created by humans. Artificial genres you can photograph include, but are not limited to: architecture (both interiors and exteriors), cities, products, technology, cars, still life, and food.

Purpose

All of us are born very creative. Designing, building, painting, cooking, writing, photographing, and the list continues. Creating is part of what we do, and capturing photos of what we make is a way to document it.

By capturing artificial objects we can display the marvel of a creative endeavor. What makes this fun is the ability to use our creativity and capture objects aesthetically from our perspective.

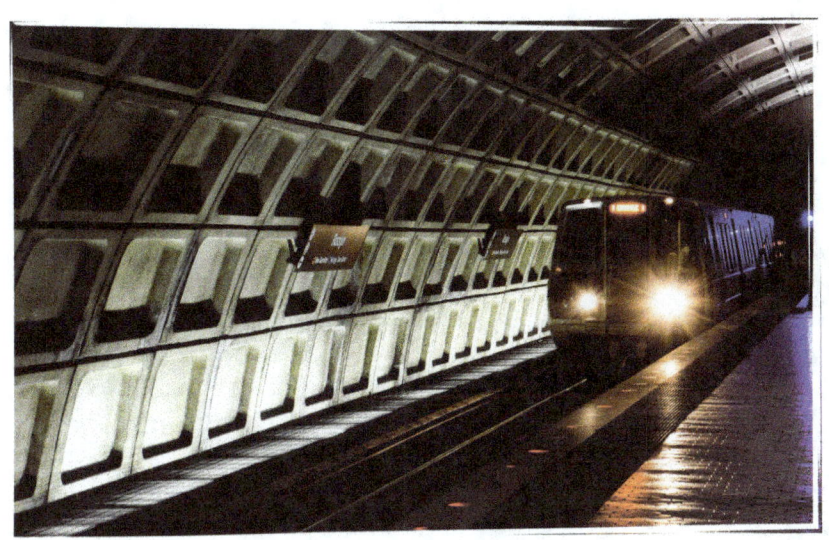

HOW TO CAPTURE ARTIFICIAL THINGS

Learning to capture great pictures of artificial objects, is learning to observe geometrics. Be able to recognize angles, shapes, lines, repetition, textures, and patterns. All elements that we use to create.

When you find yourself looking at an artificial object, try to imagine the way it was created. By noticing design features, capture it as if the object itself was meant to be photographed.

Explore every view. Find angles where geometric features are in the most visually satisfying way. Adventuring throughout a city is a fun practice to challenge your observation skills.

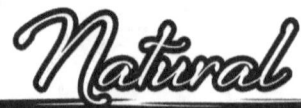

Natural

The creation of our universe is indeed marvelous. Blue skies, lightning strikes, majestic mountains, fascinating birds, galaxies, and the list never stops.
The beauty of nature is undeniable.

GENRES

Everything in the universe, except anything when humans are directly involved. Nature genres you can photograph include, but are not limited to: landscapes, wildlife, pets, flowers, sunsets, aerial, astronomy, insects, micro, scientific, ocean, and weather.

PURPOSE

The consistency with nature is that it is fascinating and marvelous. If that is our observation, then the purpose is to capture both the simplicity and sophistication of the created universe.

You can do this by capturing the action of birds, the fine grain of wood, or the vastness of a canyon. There are an unlimited possible ways you can capture nature.

Observe the parts of nature that fascinate you the most and photograph them. Discover how to capture nature in remarkable ways never seen before.

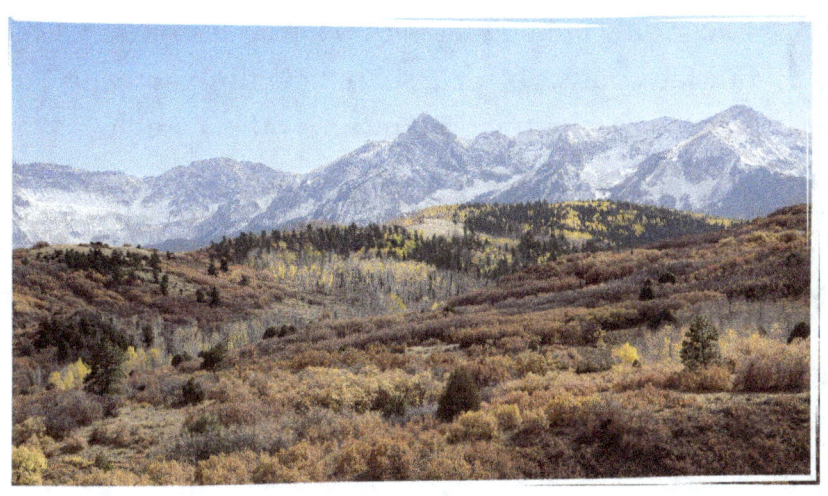

How to capture nature

The most challenging parts of nature photography are all unrelated to using your camera. It requires lots of planning, exploring areas, understanding the environment, possibly being in dangerous situations, and occasionally doing things your body does not want to do. Sometimes you might need to camp and wake up at 4 a.m. in sub-zero temperatures to get that perfect sunrise photo.

Come up with a plan of how you will capture your intended photo. Your approach is the deciding factor for gear, settings, and composition. Try not to copy what other photographers are doing, but instead, capture it based on what inspires you (page 9).

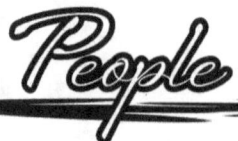

Every day, we interact with people. It is mostly what our life consists of. We share beautiful moments together, feel attraction towards others, and live through many struggles.

GENRES

All human-related things. People genres you can photograph include, but are not limited to: portraits, special events, weddings, concerts, sports, fashion, family, children, street, newborn, maternity, glamour, and journalism.

PURPOSE

People are phenomenal subjects to capture because the relationships that we create with others are precious. Amid these relationships, we experience moments of emotion. The goal should be to preserve these moments of life we are all a part of. Both the beautiful and challenging parts of life.

By doing this, you are helping document the personal history of others. Photos that can demonstrate who they are and their valuable relationships with others.

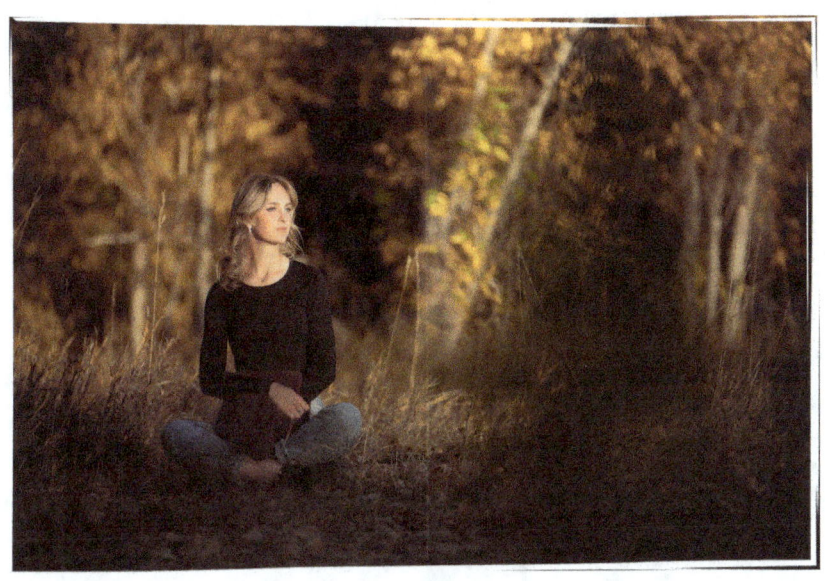

How to capture people

It should not surprise you that taking great pictures of people requires excellent people skills. That is at least eighty percent of the challenge.

For portraits, you need to observe. See people for who they are—their qualities, character, and insecurities. By observing people, you can capture not just their physical beauty but also their personality.

During events, your approach should be to capture the moments timelessly. It would be best to preserve them by staying out of the way, allowing guests to enjoy the event, and not using trendy techniques.

Yay! You
completed the book!

*(but the fun isn't
over yet)*

Appendix 1: activity log

Keep track of the activities that you complete with this log. Once you complete an activity, write down the date. Also check a star if you have practiced the topic beyond the scope of the activity (page 11).

FUNCTIONALITY

Activity	Date	Star
#1		☆
#2		☆
#3		☆
#4		☆
#5		☆
#6		☆
#7		☆
#8		☆

TECHNICAL

Activity	Date	Star
#9		☆
#10		☆
#11		☆
#12		☆
#13		☆
#14		☆
#15		☆
#16		☆
#17		☆

EXPOSURE

Activity	Date	Star
#18		☆
#19		☆
#20		☆

ARTISTRY

Activity	Date	Star
#21		☆
#22		☆
#23		☆
#24		☆
#25		☆
#26		☆
#27		☆
#28		☆
#29		☆
#30		☆

COMPOSITION

Activity	Date	Star
#31		☆
#32		☆
#33		☆
#34		☆
#35		☆

EDITING

Activity	Date	Star
#36		☆
#37		☆
#38		☆
#39		☆
#40		☆
#41		☆
#42		☆

Star aperture activity

(Do this special activity once you have checked all the stars.)

Gather all the photos captured since you started using this book. Put together an album or a calendar of all your favorite ones. It's best that you get it printed, but a digital collection of pictures is acceptable too.

Let others know about this book by sharing on your social media timeline. Writing a review online from the store you received it from is also appreciated.

Appendix 2: checklist

Before going on a trip or a photo shoot, ensure your camera is ready. You don't want to be disappointed if you forget to charge the batteries. Yes, this does happen. The following list is a bare minimum, so if you want to make a more complete checklist that fits your needs better, go for it!

1. CHARGE BATTERIES

Without power to your camera, how are you going to take pictures? Fully charging your batteries is one of the most necessary steps to ensure your camera is ready to go. Wait to check this off until your battery is inside your camera. It is also a good idea to bring extra batteries just in case.

2. PREPARE MEMORY CARDS

Import photos from your memory cards to your computer before reinserting them into the camera. Once you insert them, format the cards. If your camera supports dual card slots, consider inserting a second one and setting it in a backup role. It is also a good idea to bring extra memory cards.

Visit page 35 for more information.

3. CONFIRM SETTINGS

It's not as crucial as batteries or memory cards, but it helps make sure your camera is ready to go at any time.

▣ **Set your preferred modes:** *page 19-26*

- Metering modes: *page 19*

- Shooting modes: *page 21*

- Focusing modes: *page 23*

- Release modes: *page 25*

▣ **Set your preferred color profile:** *page 39*

▣ **Set your preferred file format:** *page 43*

▣ **Set your preferred resolution:** *page 47*

▣ **Set/sync your date and time:** *page 27*

▣ **Set your viewfinder diopter:** *adjust the diopter focus of your viewfinder to see clear sharp images without the need for glasses or eye contacts.*

Also, ensure all functions are working correctly and have no problems (page 41).

Acknowledgments

My family encouraged me to create this book.
Thank you to Gary and Janet Feil, Regan Feil, Michael
and Mariah Dupon, Toby and Sydnee Lynde, Tate
Dupon, and Sophie Dupon. Most importantly, I want
to thank my parents, Daniel and Merritt Dupon, for
supporting me, even during the biggest challenges in
life. I love you all.

I also want to thank the Larimer County 4-H program
when I was a member for eleven years during my
youth. This program allowed me to get out of my
comfort zone and gave me the confidence to do things I
wouldn't imagine myself doing, such as writing a book.

Finally, I want to thank our Creator. Without God, we
are all nothing. The multi-hue design of this book
represents the beauty of His creation. I will forever
continue to worship Him, no matter the circumstances.

*"Whatever you do, work at it with all your
heart, as working for the Lord, not for human
masters,"* - *Colossians 3:23 (NIV)*

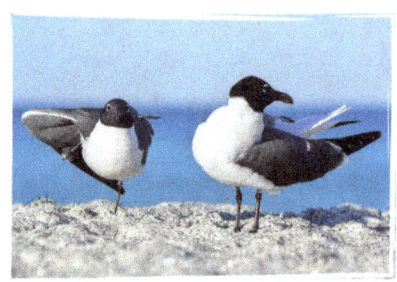
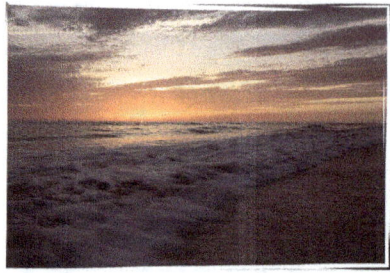

About the Writing of this Book

The inspiration for this book began during the Coronavirus pandemic in 2020. However, it wouldn't be for another few years before this book would become a written reality.

My goal when writing this book was to write something I wish that I had when learning how to take pictures. I remember when my family would take vacations to Anna Maria Island, Florida, and how I wanted to take the ultimate beach pictures.

Setting up my camera on the shore as the waves crashed into my tripod, it was those moments that I loved. At that point, I had yet to read a book about photography. I didn't care. Why would I want someone to tell me how to create my craft? I thought to myself when I was on the beach, "How should I compose?" How much I would have loved a simple and practical reference guide during those moments.

Unfortunately, I didn't have that. Instead, I continued to experiment. I discovered what worked and what didn't work, and after many years of practice, I gained enough skills to write a book. Today, it is the one you are holding right now, and without the encouragement from many amazing people, it would not exist.

About the author

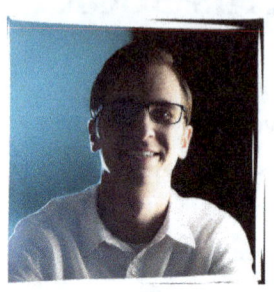

Gabriel Dupon is a professional photographer and cinematographer based in Northern Colorado. He is purely self-taught and enjoys taking pictures of people, events, wildlife, architecture, landscapes, and… *well*, basically everything!

Ever since Gabriel saved up to buy his first camera at the age of 14, he has never stopped taking pictures. When he goes out on an adventure, his aim is to capture the emotional feeling you get. Not just the beauty that you see.

DUPON
PHOTOGRAPHY

Currently, Gabriel owns Dupon Photography. He provides portrait and event services but also sells prints and photography-related products such as this book.

You can contact Gabriel Dupon by visiting his website at *www.gabrieldupon.com*

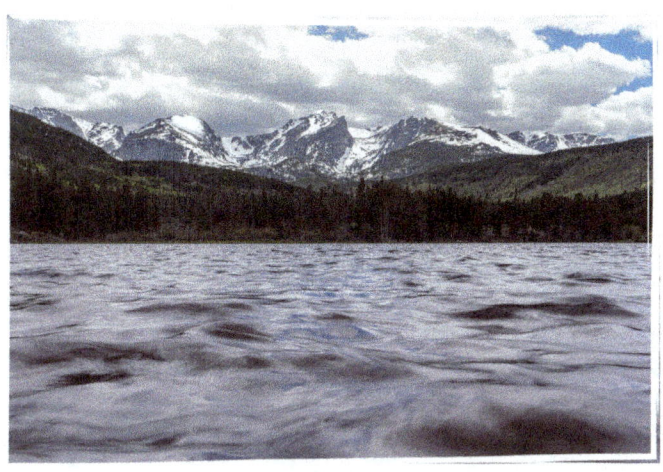

Gabriel is known for capturing the photo of Sprague Lake in Rocky Mountain National Park, which got selected for the Colorado State Driver's license in 2021. The Department of Revenue, the Colorado State Governor, and a statewide public vote chose it.

*Usually you don't start reading a
book from the back, but ok*

www.ingramcontent.com/pod-product-compliance
Lightning Source LLC
Chambersburg PA
CBHW070425290526
45791CB00005B/1844